Women of Achievement

Sandra Day O'Connor

Women of Achievement

Abigail Adams

Susan B. Anthony

Tyra Banks

Clara Barton

Hillary Rodham Clinton

Marie Curie

Ellen DeGeneres

Diana, Princess of Wales

Helen Keller

Sandra Day O'Connor

Georgia O'Keeffe

Nancy Pelosi

Rachael Ray

Eleanor Roosevelt

Martha Stewart

Venus and Serena Williams

Women of Achievement

Sandra Day
O'Connor

U.S. SUPREME COURT JUSTICE

Dennis Abrams

CHELSEA HOUSE
PUBLISHERS
An imprint of Infobase Publishing

L
J
BIO
O'CONNOR

people

SANDRA DAY O'CONNOR

Chelsea House
An imprint of Infobase Publishing
132 West 31st Street
New York, NY 10001

Library of Congress Cataloging-in-Publication Data
Abrams, Dennis, 1960-
  Sandra Day O'Connor : U.S. Supreme Court Justice / by Dennis Abrams.
      p. cm. — (Women of achievement)
  Includes bibliographical references and index.
  ISBN 978-1-60413-337-0 (hardcover)
  1. O'Connor, Sandra Day, 1930—Juvenile literature. 2. Judges—United States—Biography—Juvnile literature. 3. Women judges—United States—Biography—Juvenile literature. 4. United States. Supreme Court—Biography—Juvenile literature.
I. Title. II. Series.

  KF8745.O25A52 2009
  347.73'2634—dc22
  [B]
                                        2008055367

Chelsea House books are available at special discounts when purchased in bulk quantities for businesses, associations, institutions, or sales promotions. Please call our Special Sales Department in New York at (212) 967-8800 or (800) 322-8755.

You can find Chelsea House on the World Wide Web at http://www.chelseahouse.com

Series design by Erik Lindstrom
Cover design by Ben Peterson and Alicia Post

Printed in the United States of America

Bang EJB 10 9 8 7 6 5 4 3 2 1

This book is printed on acid-free paper.

All links and Web addresses were checked and verified to be correct at the time of publication. Because of the dynamic nature of the Web, some addresses and links may have changed since publication and may no longer be valid.

CONTENTS

1   Becoming the First   7

2   Life on the Ranch   16

3   Trying to Get Through the Door   28

4   Making Her Name   39

5   Moving Up   51

6   New Woman on the Court   62

7   Making Her Mark   74

8   Finding a Middle Ground   83

9   The Most Powerful Woman in the Nation   96

10   Life After the Court   111

Chronology   119

Notes   121

Bibliography   127

Further Resources   131

Index   132

About the Author   136

Picture Credits   136

Becoming the First

The federal government of the United States is made up of three branches with equal power: the executive, the legislative, and the judicial. Most people are aware of the president, who heads the executive branch, as well as the importance of the U.S. Senate and the House of Representatives, which make up the legislative branch. But far fewer Americans fully understand the importance of the U.S. Supreme Court, the highest court in the judiciary system. In many ways, the Supreme Court's power reaches the furthest of the three branches, because the court's decisions directly influence what goes on in the lives of all Americans.

Consider this: It was in 1954 that the Supreme Court decided the case of *Brown v. Board of Education.* (The *v.*

stands for "versus" or "against.") In its decision, the court determined that state laws establishing separate public schools for black and white students went against the U.S. Constitution and were therefore illegal. This decision helped pave the way for racial integration throughout the United States, and gave energy to the growing civil rights movement.

Or, consider these cases: In *Engel v. Vitale*, the Supreme Court decided that mandatory school prayer was unconstitutional. *Gideon v. Wainwright* established the right of a poor person to have a court-appointed attorney if he or she is unable to afford one. In *Roe v. Wade*, the court ruled that there is a constitutional right for a woman to have an abortion—a decision that remains controversial to this day. In the case of *Bush v. Gore*, one of the court's most disputed decisions in recent years, the court named George W. Bush the winner of the 2000 presidential election.

Whether it's laws concerning individual civil rights, laws regarding the environment, or laws on prosecuting the war on terror, it is the U.S. Supreme Court that has the final word. But if the court is so powerful, why do so many people know so little about it? There are several reasons for this. One is the manner in which the judges are chosen. Unlike the president, who is chosen in a national election, or members of Congress, who are elected in local and state elections, judges on the Supreme Court are named by the president and then confirmed by a vote in the U.S. Senate.

Members of Congress must defend their actions to the voters in their region in order to be reelected. Judges on the local or state level must often face voters, too. The nine Supreme Court judges, however, are chosen for life. They are never forced to justify their decisions before the American public or win the public's approval. Perhaps most importantly of all, the vast majority of the court's work is done in private. Hearings at the Supreme Court, unlike the proceedings in Congress, are not televised or broadcast on the radio. Only the people who attend a court hearing can truly know what happens there.

The decision-making process is even more private, as judges think over the facts of a case, meet, vote, and write their opinions behind the closed doors of their offices in the Supreme Court Building. The public learns how a case has been decided only after decisions are announced in court. More importantly, it is only by a careful reading of the judges' decisions that the public can know *why* the court decided a case the way it did and what the possible effects of that decision may be.

The nine Supreme Court justices have great powers to judge the legality of the actions of both the legislative and executive branches. Considering this, it is little wonder that William Howard Taft, the only American to serve both as U.S. president (1909 to 1913) and as chief justice of the Supreme Court (1921 to 1930), had this to say about the role of the court: "Presidents come and go, but the Supreme Court goes on forever."[1]

THE PRESIDENT'S DECISION

The U.S. Supreme Court is made up of eight associate justices and one head, or chief justice. One of the most crucial decisions a president can make during a term of office is naming a new justice when there is a position open. This judge is an important part of the legacy a president passes down after leaving office. The judge is someone whose decisions can direct the country for many years, long after the president is gone from office.

On March 26, 1981, Associate Justice Potter Stewart met with President Ronald Reagan's attorney general, William French Smith, to inform him of his plans to resign. The Reagan administration immediately began the search for a person to take Stewart's place. Reagan, a conservative

Republican, was eager to make his mark on a Supreme Court that he, and many others, believed was more liberal than conservative. By choosing a conservative judge to take the place of Stewart, who was more moderate, Reagan would be one justice closer to having a court with a majority of conservative judges. This is something the Republican Party had long sought.

Selecting a conservative judge was a top priority for the president, who at that point only had been in office for about two months. But there was another consideration for the administration: There never had been a female justice in the history of the court. In the years following the women's rights movement of the 1960s and 1970s, it had become obvious to many that the time had come to appoint a woman to the bench.

Indeed, in his 1980 presidential campaign, Reagan had weak support among women voters due to his opposition to the Equal Rights Amendment, his opposition to abortion, and a feeling that his promised military buildup might lead to war. Recognizing this, Reagan reached out to women voters and made what was then considered a bold promise in a speech on October 14, 1980:

> As you know, a number of false and misleading accusations have been made in this campaign. During the next three weeks, I intend to set the record straight. One of the accusations has been that I am somehow opposed to full and equal opportunities for women in America. . . . I am announcing today that one of the first Supreme Court vacancies in my administration will be filled by the most qualified woman I can find.[2]

With the resignation of Associate Justice Powell, Reagan intended to keep his word. Lyn Nofziger, a longtime

Reagan aide, wrote to the president: "I think it is imperative that you appoint a woman to the Supreme Court."[3] He only had to find the right woman for the job.

WHO WOULD HE SELECT?

A list of potential candidates was drawn up, which included U.S. Appeals Court Judge Cornelia Kennedy of Michigan, Joan Dempsey Klein, a judge on the Los Angeles Superior Court, and a little known Arizona Appeals Court judge, Sandra Day O'Connor.

On paper, O'Connor's qualifications did not make her an obvious candidate for the job. Unlike many previous nominees, she was not on a federal court or even on a top state court. For example, the court's newest judge, John Paul Stevens, had been on the U.S. Court of Appeals for five years before being chosen for the U.S. Supreme Court. Chief Justice Warren Burger had been a judge on the U.S. Court of Appeals for 13 years before being named to the high court. O'Connor was, instead, "a judge on a state intermediate court handling criminal and civil appeals."[4] As O'Connor herself noted years later, her qualifications were not obviously in line with those of a Supreme Court candidate.

O'Connor did, however, have other factors working in her favor. She was a former state senator with long-standing ties to the Republican Party. She was considered reliably conservative, but not so far to the right as to alarm the extreme left. She supported women's rights but did so without coming off as overly aggressive, which might upset some people. Perhaps most importantly, although far from being a household name, she was known and respected by men with political power: Chief Justice Burger, influential Arizona senator Barry Goldwater, and Associate Justice William Rehnquist. Her name immediately shot to the top of the list of potential candidates.

As the interview process began, she impressed everyone she met. Kenneth Starr, who was then counselor to the attorney general (and later became known for his role as the independent counsel investigating President Bill Clinton's Whitewater real-estate deal), interviewed her in the process and gave her a strong recommendation. On June 29, O'Connor met with Attorney General Smith and his wife, Jean, and made an equally strong impression, charming them both. All that was left was a meeting with the man who would make the ultimate decision: President Ronald Reagan.

THE PRESIDENT'S CHOICE

Even before meeting her, Reagan was interested in O'Connor. As biographer Joan Biskupic described it, "Her childhood on the Lazy B ranch intrigued the man who had adopted California as his home, rode horses, and chopped wood for exercise. For Reagan—the self-styled nontraditional politician—O'Connor's turn as a legislator and her relative lack of judicial experience made her more attractive than conventional nominees."[5]

The Arizona judge and the president met in the Oval Office on the morning of July 1, 1981. Years later, O'Connor remembered the meeting in an interview on an Arizona television station:

> He was pretty interested in my ranch background and fixing fences, riding horses, and a few things like that, but he did ask questions of substance as well. . . . Then it was time to go, and I said good-bye to the president and the other people who were there and left. I went to the airport to fly back to Arizona that afternoon. . . . [But] I really didn't think I would be asked to serve.[6]

President Ronald Reagan presents his Supreme Court nominee, Sandra Day O'Connor, to members of the press in the White House Rose Garden on July 15, 1981. After her confirmation by the Senate, O'Connor became the first woman to sit on the highest court in the United States.

O'Connor was wrong. Reagan did not meet with any other possible nominees. On July 7, 1981, the president walked into the White House briefing room to make his decision official. He began his speech by emphasizing the importance of his decision:

[A]s President, I have the privilege to make a certain number of nominations which have a more lasting influence on our lives, for they are the lifetime appointments of those men and women called upon to serve in the judiciary. . . . But, without doubt, the most awesome appointment . . . I can make [is] an appointment to the United States Supreme Court.

Those who sit in the Supreme Court interpret the laws of our land and truly do leave their footprints on the sands of time. Long after the policies of Presidents and Senators and Congressmen of any given era may have passed from public memory, they'll be remembered.

He then went on to state that he was sending O'Connor's name to the Senate for confirmation as associate justice of the Supreme Court, describing her in the most glowing of terms: "She is truly a person for all seasons, possessing those unique qualities of temperament, fairness, intellectual capacity, and devotion to the public good which have characterized the 101 brethren who have preceded her."[7]

With that, history was made. Sandra Day O'Connor, 51 years old, a wife, mother, politician, lawyer, and judge, was named—pending approval by the U.S. Senate—to be the first woman to sit on the U.S. Supreme Court. Few who

IN HER OWN WORDS

Although famous for being the first woman to sit on the United States Supreme Court, Sandra Day O'Connor believes her sex has little bearing on her influence as a justice. She once said:

> The power I exert on the court depends on the power of my arguments, not on my gender.

witnessed the moment ever could have guessed the impact that Reagan's decision would have. In just a matter of years, the obscure Arizona justice would become, in the words of the *Washington Post*, "the most powerful woman in the United States."[8]

How did she do it? How did the daughter of an Arizona rancher make her way from the Lazy B Ranch all the way to the U.S. Supreme Court? How did she influence the direction of the court? How did the decisions that she made change the United States and affect the lives of every U.S. citizen?

Life on the Ranch

The earliest memory is of sounds. In a place of all-encompassing silence, any sound is something to be noted and remembered. When the wind is not blowing, it is so quiet you can hear a beetle scurrying across the ground or a fly landing on a bush. Occasionally an airplane flies overhead—a high-tech intrusion penetrating the agrarian peace.

When the wind blows, as it often does, there are no trees to rustle and moan. But the wind whistles through any loose siding on the barn and causes any loose gate to bang into the fence post. It starts the windmills moving, turning, creaking.[1]

—Sandra Day O'Connor and H. Alan Day

If a person's character is established in childhood—if who they become is a reflection of the place from which they came—then it is necessary to look at the childhood years of Sandra Day O'Connor at the Lazy B Ranch. Through this, it is possible to discover the roots of the woman she ultimately became.

O'Connor's grandfather, Henry Clay Day, had established the family ranch. Day was born in Vermont in 1844 and had grown up on his father's farm in Vermont. When he turned 21, he set out on his own, gradually working his way westward. In 1880, he laid claim to land in what was then New Mexico Territory. The land was south of the Gila River, on the border of what would become the states of New Mexico and Arizona. Day's land became the Lazy B Ranch. He stocked it with cattle purchased in Mexico, which he branded with the letter *B* lying down flat—a "lazy" B.

The Lazy B Ranch was in business. Times were often difficult. Day, like other ranchers, was dependent on the land and the weather to make a living. He often had to struggle to make ends meet. He tried hiring a foreman to run the ranch while he and his family moved to Pasadena, California. Unfortunately, Day discovered that the foreman was stealing from him, so he moved his family back to the Lazy B, where he built a house and a one-room schoolhouse for his children. Harry Day, the youngest of Henry and Alice Day's children, was born in 1898.

After Henry Day found a foreman whom he trusted, the family moved back to Pasadena. Harry did well in school there, won awards in swimming, and had dreams of attending Stanford University. But when the United States entered into World War I in 1917, Harry was drafted into the army. After completing his service (without seeing any military action), Harry found himself once again putting his college dreams on hold. His father's health was failing and he was unable to keep an eye on the ranch himself. Henry sent Harry out to the Lazy B to manage the ranch. Harry was unhappy at the thought of spending time on the hot and dusty ranch, but he did as his father asked.

Although he only expected to stay for a few months, the day never came when Harry could escape the ranch. When his father died in 1921, Harry gave up his dream of attending college and having a career in order to get the family business out of debt and running smoothly. Life was hard and lonely for Harry, but his life would change with a trip to El Paso, Texas, to purchase some new bulls for the Lazy B.

WHEN HARRY MET ADA

Her name was Ada Mae Wilkey, and she was the 23-year-old daughter of W.W. Wilkey, a successful cattle rancher and businessman, and Mamie Scott Wilkey. Ada was far from the typical rancher's daughter. She played the piano well, had graduated from the University of Arizona (a rare accomplishment for a woman born in 1904), and, rather surprisingly, already had been married and divorced. Back home with her parents, she taught school, played bridge, and was an active participant in the social activities typical of her class and upbringing.

When Harry Day, with little money and no college education, appeared at her house one evening for supper after doing business with her father, it was love at first sight for them both. The night they met, the couple stayed up late talking and hated to say good-bye. Separated by many miles of difficult traveling, the two began writing to each other daily.

After three months of such correspondence, the couple eloped to Las Cruces, New Mexico, where a justice of the peace married them on September 19, 1927. Ada Mae gave up the life of a successful rancher's daughter to live with Harry Day on a struggling ranch with no running water or electricity, located 35 miles (55 kilometers) from the nearest

HARRY DAY AND ADA MAE WILKEY

During the three months they were apart, separated by many miles of difficult traveling, Sandra Day O'Connor's parents began writing long, passionate letters to each other. The correspondence began with Harry, who wrote Ada a letter immediately after their first meeting

> . . . to tell you . . . how you have changed a dull, dreary life into something worthwhile—and to tell you again that I love you more than anything in the world and that I have never felt the same way toward anyone I have ever known before. It seems I have loved you always, dear, and you have always been mine.

to which Ada Mae responded,

> I would have died, I do believe, if your precious letter had not come this morning. And it surely made up for all my impatience for its arrival—it is the sweetest treasure I have ever had and am going to wear the pages out reading and re-reading every single word. Oh, how I miss you, my beloved. I love you until it hurts and I am so lonesome for you!*

The couple was happily married for almost 57 years, until Harry's death in 1984.

---

* Sandra Day O'Connor and H. Alan Day, *Lazy B: Growing Up On a Cattle Ranch in the American Southwest.* New York: Random House, 2003, pp. 42–43.

town of Lordsburg. The newlyweds shared the house with several cowboys who slept on the porch. Ada Mae never looked back. She and Harry lived on that ranch for more than 50 years.

SANDRA DAY

The couple's first child, Sandra, was born on March 26, 1930. For the birth, Ada Mae Day left the ranch and traveled 200 miles (320 km) to her family home in El Paso, so she could be near a hospital. Although Harry and Ada Mae were delighted to be parents, their firstborn arrived at a particularly difficult time.

The United States was in the midst of the Great Depression. Banks across the country had closed, hundreds of thousands of people were out of work, and life on the ranch, already hard, grew more difficult. Even the weather turned against the ranchers, as drought gripped the Southwest time and again. Times were so bad that, when Sandra was just two, Harry could not afford to buy feed for the cattle and was forced to try and find a buyer for more than 200 painfully thin animals. As O'Connor described it years later in *Lazy B*, the one man who came out to look at the cattle was shocked by their condition, saying, "I wouldn't take that bunch of cows if you gave them to me. It wouldn't be worth the shipping charges."[2]

Somehow, the family survived. Harry Day made every penny stretch as far as it could. Ada Mae, in the meantime, strove to keep the family's lifestyle above that of the usual ranch house: Ada Mae always wore dresses and stockings. Gourmet meals were served on good china. She kept a flower garden, played her piano, and subscribed to magazines such as *Vogue* and *House Beautiful*.

She also introduced her daughter to the beauty of nature. The two would go on walks around the ranch, and Ada Mae would show Sandra the native plant and animal life, and together they would look for arrowheads and pieces of Native American pottery. Ada Mae also taught her daughter how to read by age four. As Joan Biskupic explained in her biography *Sandra Day O'Connor*, Ada Mae "instilled in her daughter a love of music and a gift for entertaining, along with a talent for cards and a spirit of adventure."[3] All of these skills would prove handy to Sandra throughout the course of her life and career.

While her mother nurtured the family, her father taught Sandra how to work on the ranch and about the difficulties of life. By the time Sandra was eight years old, she knew how to mend a fence, ride a horse, shoot a rifle, and drive a tractor. Although he was always a loving father, Harry Day could also be hard to please. A job well done was nothing to be celebrated or praised; it was something that was expected.

Sandra, even at an early age, had to work hard and go the extra mile to earn her father's approval. In her memoir, O'Connor recalled a time when she was young and noticed that the back porch's screen door needed to be painted. She offered to do it, and after hours of careful work—sanding it down, carefully taping over the metal hinges, and painting the newly smooth wood—the job was completed.

That night over dinner, Sandra asked her father if he had seen the screen door. "Yes. Did you clean the paintbrush and put the lid on the paint can and put it away?" "Of course," she replied. "That's all right then," replied her father. "And that was all the thanks I received,"[4] Sandra recalled. But she knew that, despite her father's lack of praise, he had thought the job was done properly. That's what counted.

Winning her father's praise was nearly impossible, but in trying to win it—in always trying to do the best job she possibly could do—Sandra developed skills that served her well her entire life. As Biskupic tells it, by the time Sandra left the ranch, she had learned "a lesson in the virtues of hard work, a talent for maneuvering among tough characters, and a competitive drive that sustained her through a journey no woman had taken before."[5]

GOING AWAY FOR SCHOOL

Sandra found herself forced to leave home sooner than she had possibly expected. The ranch itself was miles from anyone and anything, so Sandra's first friends were the cowboys who worked the ranch; her beloved horse, Chico; and an ever-changing assortment of pets, including a tame bobcat imaginatively named "Bob." It was, in some ways, an ideal existence—so much so that O'Connor has talked about it lovingly her entire life.

Living in such a remote area also made it nearly impossible to find quality local education. At the age of six, Sandra was sent away to El Paso, where she would live with her maternal grandmother, Mamie Wilkey. There she would attend the Radford School for Girls, a school noted for its tough-minded approach to education.

For Sandra, the move to El Paso was traumatic. She loved the ranch and her parents and could not understand why they would send her away from home. She worried that they did not want her there. She was able to go home at Christmas, at Easter, and for summer vacation, but always dreaded returning to her grandmother's house. Her homesickness was so sharp that she said in a 1980 interview, "I dislike El Paso to this day, largely because I was homesick."[6]

If life at the Lazy B was isolated geographically, life at her grandmother's house felt isolating in other ways. Most of the girls at the Radford School lived at the school and came from well-to-do families. Sandra Day felt out of place among them. When asked years later about her memories of Day, the former dean of the school said, "She loved riding horses and she got homesick for her family."[7] One factor that helped to ease Sandra's loneliness was the presence of her cousin Flournoy, who also was living at Grandma Wilkey's while attending the Radford School.

By this time, Sandra was no longer an only child. Her sister, Ann, was born in 1938 and her brother, Alan, was born in 1939. Sandra enjoyed getting to know them during her stays at the ranch, but she still longed to come home permanently. She got her wish in eighth grade, when her parents finally agreed to let her live at home and commute daily to school.

It was a difficult trip to make. The closest school was in Lordsburg, 20 miles (32 km) from the ranch, near the Arizona–New Mexico border. Early each morning, either Harry or Ada Mae Day would drive their daughter 8 miles (13 km) to a highway intersection, where she would wait for a bus. It was a one-hour bus ride from there to school, and then a reverse trip back that got her home after sunset. One year of this was enough for her parents. The next year, Sandra returned to El Paso and the Radford School for Girls. (Interestingly, the time she spent commuting to school influenced her legal thinking. During her confirmation hearings, O'Connor referred to this period as a lesson against the use of forced busing to help achieve racial integration in public schools.)

After finishing at Radford, Sandra transferred to El Paso's Austin High School, from which she graduated at the age of 16. The summer before she graduated, though, she had an experience at the ranch that left a lasting impression on her. It involved lunch, cattle branding, and winning her father's approval.

Sandra Day O'Connor (*right*) is shown in a photo taken on the family ranch at Easter 1940. Her mother, Ada Mae Day, holds her brother Alan; her sister Ann is in the middle.

"YOU NEED TO EXPECT ANYTHING OUT HERE."

The spring cattle roundup was over, but Harry Day thought they had missed some cattle near Antelope Well. He planned to spend a few days there gathering up the cattle with unbranded calves. Ada Mae planned to make the lunches for the crews while they were there, and Sandra offered to take the men their lunches each day.

The night before, Ada Mae and Sandra prepared the men's lunch: a big pot roast with green chilies, scalloped potatoes, green beans, and an applesauce cake. It was a two-and-a-half-hour drive to where the men were working, and Sandra left at seven in the morning to be sure to get there on time. She was just 15 years old.

Traveling south in an old pickup truck fully loaded with lunch and other supplies, Sandra set off driving down old dirt roads. Suddenly, the truck began to feel wobbly. Sandra got out to see what was wrong and saw that the left rear tire had gone flat. She wasn't worried—she knew how to change a tire. But it wasn't going to be as easy as she thought.

After putting large rocks behind the front wheels so they wouldn't roll, she jacked up the truck. To her dismay, she discovered that the lug nuts that connected the wheel to the truck had rusted. They wouldn't budge, no matter how hard she tried to turn them. Knowing that there would be no one coming down that road, she had to figure out how to fix it on her own. Lowering the truck on the jack, she tried to loosen the lug nuts by jumping up and down on the lug wrench. It worked. The nuts cracked open, and Sandra was able to remove the flat tire and replace it with the spare. An hour later, bone tired and drenched with sweat, she backed out onto the road.

It was close to 11 A.M. when she arrived at the men's camp, an hour past their usual lunchtime. The men already had begun branding the cattle, and Sandra set to work building a fire to make coffee and to reheat the food. It was nearly 1:30 P.M. by the time the men were able to sit down to eat. Sandra was eager to tell her father how she had solved the problem with the truck, but Harry Day was too disappointed with his daughter to listen, as she recounted in *Lazy B*:

> "You're late," said DA [her father's nickname]. "I know," I said. "I had a flat tire on the other side of Robbs' Well and had to change it." "You should have started earlier," said DA. "Sorry, DA, I didn't expect a flat." "You need to expect anything out here." . . .
>
> I had expected a word of praise for changing the tire. But, to the contrary, I realized that only one thing was expected: an on-time lunch. No excuses accepted.[8]

No excuses accepted. Sandra Day learned many important life lessons growing up on the Lazy B, as Scott Bales wrote in his *Stanford Law Review* tribute to O'Connor:

> Growing up on the Lazy B indelibly influenced O'Connor's character and perspective. She has noted that on the ranch, "no task was too small to be done as well as possible. No task was too large to be undertaken." She also recalled that her family's ability to sustain the ranch for more than 100 years reflected "planning, patience, skill, and endurance." Of the cowboys who lived on the Lazy B, she wrote: "[They] did whatever job was required. They met the unexpected as though they'd known about it all

along. They never complained, and they made the best of everything along the way." Similar qualities of self-confident determination and commitment in the face of challenges have long characterized O'Connor herself.[9]

There was one additional lesson she learned from her father. When it came to politics, Harry Day was a conservative. During the Great Depression, President Franklin Delano Roosevelt used government programs to help those in need. Because Day believed in self-reliance and in a limited role for the federal government, he hated Roosevelt's policies. Political discussions around the kitchen table were a common feature in the Day household. From her father, Sandra developed a distrust of a powerful federal government.

By the mid-1940s, with the Lazy B on sound financial footing, Harry Day was able to send his oldest daughter to college. The year was 1946. Sandra was about to embark on a journey that would enable her to fulfill her father's dreams, and then go beyond them in ways he never could have imagined.

Trying to Get Through the Door

Like her father, Sandra Day wanted to attend Stanford University in Palo Alto, California. But unlike her father, who was unable to go to college due to his family responsibilities, Sandra Day entered Stanford in 1946. She was ready to prove herself in a world much larger than that of the Lazy B and the Radford School for Girls.

Sandra was only 16 years old, younger than the usual college freshman. Fresh from the isolated world of the Lazy B, Sandra was enrolling at a university with more than 7,000 students, 2,000 of who were women. With her cowgirl ways, Sandra was concerned that she wouldn't fit in.

She need not have worried. Living in a dormitory with other girls from rural areas, Sandra quickly fell into the rituals of campus life. Even her dorm mates were impressed when, after the first school dance, a "cute" guy with a red convertible drove her back to the dorm. She was served well by the skills she had learned at the ranch and at her grandmother's house: her competitive streak, her need to please others, and her desire to do her best.

She quickly settled in academically as well. She entered Stanford planning to study economics, to learn the theories behind the reality she had seen at home as she watched her father struggle to make the ranch profitable. While taking an undergraduate class in business law, Sandra encountered the legendary professor Harry Rathbun. Professor Rathbun, known for his ability to inspire his students, had an enormous impact on Sandra's life.

The lesson learned from Rathbun was that the individual had a responsibility to the community. In Charles Lane's article "The Professor Who Lit the Spark," O'Connor recalled that he "was the first person ever to speak in my presence of how an individual can make a difference; how a single caring person can effectively help determine the course of events."[1] She went on to say in a later interview, "I had never heard that before. He wanted to persuade us to go out into the world and do something. Because of that professor, I went to law school."[2] For Sandra Day, whose parents always had stood outside the community and relied solely upon themselves, Rathbun's words were an eye-opener.

In 1950, after receiving her bachelor's degree in economics, magna cum laude (high honors), Day made the decision to continue her education at Stanford Law School. Her parents always had hated having to rely on attorneys for legal matters regarding the ranch. They thought that having a lawyer in the family was probably a good thing, since it would relieve them of the need for outside help. They therefore agreed to pay for their eldest daughter's law school.

1948

1950

1950

1950

Above, several photos of Sandra Day O'Connor taken during her college years.

BECOMING AN ATTORNEY

Sandra Day was only 19 when she finished her undergraduate work and entered law school, one of just five women in her class. Among her classmates was 25-year-old William Rehnquist, whose education had been delayed by World

War II. Rehnquist—who years later would become the chief justice of the U.S. Supreme Court—was impressed by Day's ability to ask questions without fear of being ridiculed. This is a remarkable feat even today, when women in law schools often find themselves intimidated by male professors and classmates.

In a 2007 interview with Erin Wiley, co-president of the Cornell Law School chapter of Ms. JD, a group focusing on the empowerment of women in the law, O'Connor discussed how she coped with the pressures of law school:

> I had no strategy when I went to law school. I just wanted to try to do well and get decent grades. If there were any type of strategy it would have been to try to understand what the professor was trying to teach, to take adequate notes, and to study hard for the exams. I had no strategy for participation in class. The professors wanted every student to contribute and they would call on every student. If you didn't volunteer you were apt to be called on anyway. We had to be ready to respond and that

IN HER OWN WORDS

In an interview with Jan Crawford Greenburg, O'Connor discussed the changing role of women in American society:

> Young women today often have very little appreciation for the real battles that took place to get women where they are today in this country. I don't know how much history young women today know about those battles.

meant that you had to do the reading and work in preparation for that class because you never knew when you would be asked to contribute something. I suppose preparation is the best strategy.[3]

Indeed, preparation was the best strategy. When she graduated from law school in 1952, Sandra Day was third in her class of 102 students, just two places behind Rehnquist. In just six years, she had earned two degrees, had served as an editor of the *Stanford Law Review*, and had received membership in the honor society Order of the Coif—one of the highest honors a law student can receive.

William Rehnquist and Sandra Day, two future Supreme Court justices, had worked together on the *Stanford Law Review*, a legal journal that contains articles on matters of law written by students, professors, and judges. Students are selected to work on the journal based on a competitive exercise that tests candidates on their editing skills and legal writing ability. Working on the journal is a major achievement in the career of any aspiring attorney. For young Sandra Day to make the *Stanford Law Review* was a testament to both her ability and her ambition.

Rehnquist and Day were more than just classmates and members of the *Law Review*. The pair also dated briefly, but soon realized that their attraction was more intellectual than romantic. This decision was confirmed when Day met the man who became the love of her life, John Jay O'Connor III.

TWO WORLDS MEET

While Day's family had to work hard on the Lazy B to make ends meet, O'Connor came from a different kind of family. The grandson of Irish immigrants who went on to help found St. Francis Hospital in San Francisco, he grew up in a well-to-do household. Even in the depths of

Two future Supreme Court justices, Sandra Day O'Connor (*second from left, first row*) and William Rehnquist (*back row, farthest left*), pose for a photograph with their Law Review Board of Editors (1950–1951) at Stanford. Rehnquist would be appointed to the Supreme Court by President Richard M. Nixon; O'Connor by President Reagan.

the Depression, the family continued to be able to afford hired help.

But John O'Connor was no spoiled rich kid. As Joan Biskupic points out in her biography of Sandra Day O'Connor, he had drive and ambition, writing notes to himself while in law school as reminders to stay focused. Those attributes, along with his Irish good looks and a strong sense of humor, endeared him to Day.

The pair met while working on the *Stanford Law Review*, proofreading and checking the citations in an article. After hours of research in the library, O'Connor suggested to Day that the two take a break at Dinah's Shack, a popular local diner. Years later, she joked, "Beware of proofreading over a glass of beer. It can result in unexpected alliances."[4] One date was all it took. The two became an immediate couple and, according to John, went out 41 nights in a row. Things were clearly serious, and it was time for Sandra Day to take John O'Connor home to meet her parents.

MEETING DA

It was on spring break in 1952 when Day brought city boy O'Connor to the Lazy B and gave him his first encounter with life on the ranch. After bringing O'Connor to the house to meet her mother, it was time for him to meet a somewhat more formidable figure, Harry Day. As O'Connor said in a later interview, "You had to prove to Harry Day that you were the right kind of person before he would really open up. In addition, it was clear that Sandra was his treasure."[5]

The story of the first meeting between Harry Day and John O'Connor is a classic, one that has become family legend. Sandra Day O'Connor later recounted it in *Lazy B*:

> DA was aware that we were there, but he did not stop the work to say hello. He nodded at us briefly but continued to use the branding irons. Finally, he motioned John and me over and said, "Hello. Glad to see you. This must be John. We're a little busy right now, John. We'll be through after a while." Then DA went to the corral fence and took down a piece of baling wire that was hanging there. He straightened it out and reached into a dirty-looking bucket and pulled out a couple of bloody testicles that Rastus [a ranch hand] had tossed in there after castrating some calves. DA trimmed them a bit

with his pocketknife, then put them on the baling wire and placed them in the branding fire, where the "mountain oysters," as we called them, sizzled and cooked. DA turned them to cook all sides, then brought the baling-wire skewer over to John and said, "Here, John, try some of these." John gulped a bit and said, "Sure, Mr. Day." He plucked one of the "oysters" off the wire and popped it in his mouth. "Umm, pretty good," he said.

Welcome to the Lazy B, I thought. There is nothing like a gracious introduction to ranch life.[6]

John O'Connor had passed Harry Day's first test. For the next few days, Sandra took John riding on the roundup, introduced him to the people of the ranch, and let him get to know the place she loved more than anywhere else in the world.

That summer, just months after their first meeting, John O'Connor and Sandra Day announced their engagement. They were married on December 20, 1952, at the Lazy B, six months after Day graduated from Stanford. The 200 guests at the wedding witnessed Sandra Day walk down the aisle of the ranch's newly built barn, which was decorated with pinion tree boughs and mistletoe.

Sandra Day, now Sandra Day O'Connor, was married to a man she not only loved, but one who provided her with a social status and financial security that she had never before enjoyed. For many women in the 1950s, this would have been enough, and they would have been content in the role of wife and mother. But Sandra Day O'Connor was not like many women. She had ambitions of her own. She would soon discover, however, that talent, ambition, and a law degree from a top school sometimes weren't enough to make it in what was still a man's world.

KNOCKING ON DOORS

After honeymooning in Acapulco, Mexico, the couple returned to Stanford so that John could finish his final semester of law school. Armed with her degree, Sandra Day O'Connor did what every new law graduate did—set out to find a full-time legal position at a good law firm. Her task was more difficult than she had anticipated.

In 1872, the U.S. Supreme Court agreed with a decision by the Supreme Court of Illinois that denied Myra Bradwell admission to the state lawyer's association (called the bar) for the reason that she was female. Justice Joseph P. Bradley wrote: "The natural and proper timidity and delicacy which belongs to the female sex evidently unfits it for many of the occupations of civil life."[7] It wasn't until 1890—after years of battles—that Bradwell finally was admitted to the Illinois State Bar Association. (And it wasn't until 1971 and the case of *Reed v. Reed* that the Supreme Court overturned its previous opinion and declared that discrimination on the basis of a person's sex was unconstitutional. The attorney arguing that case was a young Ruth Bader Ginsburg, who 22 years later, would join O'Connor on the Supreme Court as its second female justice.)

By the 1950s, opportunities for female attorneys had improved, but not by much. In 1950, for example, out of a total of 180,461 employed lawyers and judges in the United States, only 6,256 were women, according to U.S. Census figures. (That number climbed to more than 250,000 women by 2000—one quarter of the legal profession—even though women made up 44 percent of all law school students.) Even in 1952, being a female attorney was still an oddity. O'Connor would have to overcome the bias that had been built up over generations by male attorneys in order to forge her legal career.

O'Connor interviewed with many top California firms. Despite the fact that she had graduated third in her class and had sat on the *Stanford Law Review*, she was unable to find work. Adding insult to injury, the one job offer she did receive, from the firm of Gibson, Dunn, and Crutcher, was as a legal secretary. She declined the position.

Instead, O'Connor accepted an offer to work as a deputy county attorney in the San Mateo County attorney's office, where she handled civil cases such as divorce, breach of contract, and negligence. These were non-criminal cases involving a dispute among individuals, or an individual and a company, or two companies. The job, though it didn't last long, gave her experience as a public lawyer, which she greatly appreciated.

In 1953, after graduating from law school, John O'Connor was drafted into the U.S. Army and sent to Germany, where he worked in the Judge Advocate General Corps. Sandra went with him and found work as a civilian attorney for the U.S. Quartermaster Corps in the city of Frankfurt. The work was not particularly time-consuming, and on weekends, Sandra and John were able to travel extensively across Europe. During this time O'Connor developed a love for skiing that has lasted her a lifetime.

When John's military service ended, it was time to return home. This time though, home did not mean the Lazy B or Palo Alto. John and Sandra Day O'Connor would be starting a home of their own, and Sandra was going to become a mother.

STARTING A FAMILY

The year was 1957. The young couple decided that, rather than return to California, they would set up a home in Phoenix, Arizona. There were many advantages to making such a move. With a population of just a little more than 100,000 in 1950, the two new attorneys had a better chance of making an impact in Phoenix and getting involved with the community there, compared with their chances of doing so in one of the larger, more established cities of California. (San Francisco, for example, had a population at the time of well more than 700,000.) In addition, living in Phoenix put the couple within an easy traveling distance to the Lazy B—still Sandra's favorite place, and already equipped with loving grandparents.

Many other young couples like the O'Connors were moving into Phoenix as well. William Rehnquist and his wife, Nan, also had settled there. By 1960, the population of Phoenix had exploded to more than 439,000 people. As was the case in many cities in the so-called "Sun Belt," expansion was occurring at a furious rate. With population growth came the kind of growing political power that Sandra Day O'Connor wanted for her state.

The O'Connor family's first home in Phoenix was an apartment. Despite its small size, they equipped the space with a ping-pong table for late-night competitions. Early on, the pair caught the eye of *Arizona Republic* magazine, which published an article about what was then a true oddity—husband and wife lawyers. In describing O'Connor's work in San Mateo County, the magazine focused more on her looks than her intelligence: "She probably was the youngest and, undoubtedly, the prettiest assistant DA to be found anywhere."[8]

On October 5, 1957, John O'Connor and Sandra Day O'Connor were sworn into the Arizona bar. Their first son, Scott, was born just three days later. John O'Connor already had found a position with the law firm Fennemore Craig, one of the oldest and largest firms in the Southwest. But Sandra Day O'Connor still was running into the same problem she had found in California: None of the city's firms were interested in hiring a female attorney. O'Connor, now faced with the additional responsibility of caring for a newborn, would have to find a way to make her own career.

Making Her Name

It is important to remember that in 1957, the women's liberation movement was still a decade away. The traditional role of a woman was to marry, to tend house, and to have children. Just a quarter of all married women worked, and they only worked in what were generally accepted jobs for women: as teachers, nurses, or secretaries. Women in other professions were still a rarity then, despite the fact that they had shown they could work in a wide variety of fields during World War II (1939–1945). This is no longer the case today, thanks in large part to the trailblazing example of women such as Sandra Day O'Connor. Today, doors now are open for women in the law and in most other professions.

But in 1957, those doors were still closed. In order to practice law, O'Connor decided to open up her own law

firm with a University of Michigan graduate named Tom
Tobin in the spring of 1958. Their firm was in a Phoenix
shopping center that also was occupied by a grocery store,
a television repair shop, a liquor store, and a dry clean-
ing business. It was a long way from the prestigious law
firm at which her husband worked, but at least she was
practicing law.

The cases the two aspiring attorneys accepted were
basic, as O'Connor described in an interview with the
Phoenix History Project. If local merchants needed a lease
drawn up or advice concerning a contract, the firm could
handle that. If people in the area had problems involving
marriage or divorce, or if they had landlord-tenant problems, the lawyer duo would handle that as well. And, in the
days before the establishment of a public defender's office,
O'Connor and Tobin could go down to the courtroom and
wait around, hoping that a judge might appoint them to a
criminal case, for which they would receive the grand sum
of $25 for their services.

O'Connor kept herself busy in other ways, as well, by
going out and actively campaigning for local Republican
candidates. By working for other Republicans, she soon
found herself gaining appointments to sit on county boards
and panels.

And of course, on top of her legal work and growing political activity, she was also a wife and mother. The
O'Connors had hired a babysitter for Scott, so Sandra was
able to focus on her work, but she also knew that finding
a way to balance her career and motherhood was difficult.
She discussed the competing demands placed on women in
her interview with Ms. JD:

> [I]t sure isn't easy, and some women have made a
> choice not to have a family, some women have made
> a choice to get established in their work or profession

first before having a family. I decided early on that I would like to have children and I got married at a fairly early age. We were twenty-two when we got married, and I have never regretted the choice to have children, to have a family, but it was not easy. I have never had time for my own private pursuits because every moment of every day was taken up either with my work or my family. I wouldn't change it but it's not easy and not everyone is going to tolerate so much to do as that. It's like having two full time jobs. Some women can do that, others find it too stressful. I don't think time and distance has made that a lot easier but it can be done and at the end of the day I thought it was worthwhile.[1]

Of course, unlike millions of other working women, O'Connor had the benefit of a husband who could support the family if they so chose, as well as the luxury of having a full-time babysitter. After the birth of their second child, Brian, in 1960, the family's long-time babysitter moved away,

IN HER OWN WORDS

Sandra Day O'Connor knows that her success came through not only her own efforts, but with the help and support of her family and close friends. She once noted:

> We don't accomplish anything in this world alone . . . and whatever happens is the result of the whole tapestry of one's life and all the weavings of individual threads from one to another that creates something.

and O'Connor found herself unable to find a replacement. Day care, so common today, was still a rarity back then. O'Connor found herself facing a situation common to many other women: She had to sacrifice her career for her family. She left the law firm she had founded with Tom Tobin, and for the next five years concentrated on being a mother.

NETWORKING

Although O'Connor was no longer working as a lawyer, she was still active politically, first becoming a precinct commit-teeman and then county vice-chairman for the Republican Party. She also kept busy writing wills and serving as a trustee for the Federal Bankruptcy Court, but always with the understanding that she would be able to work on those cases from home.

O'Connor was fortunate that she had a husband who understood her need to work while raising children. It also helped that John O'Connor's career was flourishing. He was successful at Fennemore, and he became active among Phoenix's rapidly growing political power players. He joined the Young Republicans and the Phoenix Rotary Club, and he became a member of the board of the local United Way. Sandra was working her way up the social ladder as well, quickly becoming a force to be reckoned with in the Phoenix Junior League, the top organization for ambitious wives of ambitious husbands.

By this time, the O'Connors had left their earlier apartment for a white adobe house in the Phoenix sub-urb of Paradise Valley, and they turned their home into a gathering point for Arizona's young Republicans. While entertaining or hosting political fund-raisers and Election Night parties, Sandra Day O'Connor was in her element, preparing gourmet meals for an ever-expanding group of Arizona's power elite.

Arizona Republicans were on their way to becoming *the* dominant political party in the state. The Democrats, once in the majority, found themselves outnumbered as tens of thousands of young conservatives such as O'Connor and Rehnquist, in addition to conservative senior citizens, flocked there to enjoy the state's warm weather and rapidly expanding economy. The O'Connors had returned to the state just as their political beliefs and those of their new home state were falling into synch.

STARTING UP THE POLITICAL LADDER

In her usual hardworking way, O'Connor made herself known in Republican political circles. She worked to support the 1958 Senate reelection bid of conservative Republican Barry Goldwater. Senator Goldwater won reelection handily, and with his victory came greater national recognition for Goldwater. In 1964, Goldwater, the leading conservative Republican in the nation, won his party's nomination for the presidency, but he lost the general election in a landslide to the Democratic candidate, President Lyndon B. Johnson.

Despite Goldwater's loss, O'Connor's efforts for the campaign strengthened her relationship with the state Republican Party's most powerful players. This connection paid off just a year later when Arizona State Attorney General Bob Pickrell appointed her as an assistant state attorney general.

As assistant attorney general, O'Connor was able to broaden her contacts within the Republican party. Her hard work and diligence soon made her an invaluable employee—so invaluable, in fact, that she negotiated a deal that allowed her to work part-time. "I did the best I could in order that they would feel that I was indispensable," she told the Phoenix History Project. "Then when I told them that I very much needed to work only part-time and asked them if they wouldn't work out an arrangement for me, they then agreed to do it because, by then, they decided that they needed me even on my terms."[2]

Despite her work, O'Connor still ran the household. She planned all the meals and hired the household help. The two oldest O'Connor children were now in school, and a capable babysitter was found for the youngest son, Jay, born in 1962. Even after long hours of work, O'Connor did not allow herself to rest after dinner. She would either finish work from the office, or go out and play tennis with her husband. As youngest son Jay described it, "My mom would rarely flop down on the couch."[3]

Four years later, in 1969, O'Connor was ready for her next move. President Richard M. Nixon selected Arizona State Senator Isabel Burgess to be on the National Transportation Safety Board. This opened up a seat in the state senate, one that O'Connor wanted. She was friends with both Burgess and the county board supervisors who would be making the appointment. She actively campaigned for the position.

To no one's great surprise, she got the job. O'Connor quickly established herself as a power to be reckoned with, winning the chairmanship of the senate's State, County and Municipal Affairs Committee, as well as seats on both the Appropriations Committee and the Judiciary Committee. As O'Connor herself admitted in a later interview, she was, in part, benefiting from the growing women's movement, which demanded that women play a greater role in politics and government. Once again, she was in the right place at the right time.

The wife and mother who had been nibbling on the fringes of political life was now a power player herself. Many years later, O'Connor, in her book *The Majesty of the Law: Reflections of a Supreme Court Justice*, described the need for women to gain power in order to bring about change. "Power [is] the ability to do. For both men and women, the first step in getting power is to become visible to others—and then to put on an impressive show."[4] This, of course, was what Sandra Day O'Connor set out to do.

PROVING HER WORTH

Despite advances in the women's movement, politics in Arizona and throughout the nation in the late 1960s and early 1970s was still a man's game. Between 1950 and 1970, only three women served in the Arizona State Senate. (Some strides were made during the years 1970 to 1990, when a grand total of 17 women served in the Arizona State Senate.) To many of her colleagues, the idea that a woman could be both feminine and intelligent was something of a shock. As Joan Biskupic points out, "She was clever in a way that most men, in 1971, did not expect from their female counterparts."[5]

O'Connor herself was aware that her role as state senator was still a relatively unique one for a woman, and she was supportive of the women's rights movement. Indeed, when President Nixon appointed her old friend William Rehnquist to the U.S. Supreme Court in 1971 to take the seat vacated by retiring associate justice John Marshall Harlan II, O'Connor's happiness at her friend's success was mixed with her disappointment that a woman had not been offered the seat. In the United States at that time, there were 8,750 judges, of which only 300 were women. And only eight of them were sitting on federal courts.

Along with her duties in the state senate, O'Connor worked in other ways to advance her political career. In addition to the parties she threw for Arizona's political and business elite, she was appointed to the board of directors of the Heard Museum of Native American Art and to the board of trustees of her old university, Stanford. She also campaigned for the Republican Party and its candidates, serving as state co-chair for Richard Nixon's 1972 reelection campaign. She worked tirelessly on his behalf, using her skills as an "organizer of people and a synthesizer of facts"[6] to bring together as many different groups as she could in support of the president.

When Nixon won the state with 67 percent of the vote, O'Connor's reputation within the party continued to grow. She began to be seen as having a political future beyond the Arizona state lines. As Nixon's regional director, Thomas C. Reed, said in a letter to Anne Armstrong at the Republican National Committee, "She is an attorney, attractive, about my age, with more brains and energy than can be utilized in all of Arizona."[7]

Having easily won reelection in 1970 and 1972, O'Connor was rewarded by her fellow Republican state senators, who elected her as their Senate majority leader over two members who had more experience. In just three years, O'Connor had risen to the second highest position in the Arizona state senate. Despite this, she constantly faced sexism in the state senate. As one long-time political reporter said, "It's too bad Sandra isn't a man. She would really go places."[8]

Others, however, appreciated her worth. In the words of *Arizona Republic* political editor Bernie Wynn, "'Sandy,' as she is known around the Capitol, is a sharp gal. She is articulate, has a steel-trap mind, boundless energy, and a large measure of common sense."[9] O'Connor would need all of those skills in her new role as majority leader.

ROE V. WADE

On January 22, 1973, the U.S. Supreme Court announced its decision in the case of *Roe v. Wade*, a decision whose impact has been deeply felt for more than 35 years. In this

An estimated 5,000 people march around the Minnesota Capitol building to protest the U.S. Supreme Court's *Roe v. Wade* decision, which legalized abortion across the United States in 1973.

case, the Supreme Court ruled on the legality of abortion. For years, the court had found that there exists a "right of privacy," a space within the private lives of U.S. citizens in which the government may not interfere. This right, although it is not specifically spelled out in the Constitution, is thought to be suggested in the Ninth Amendment and Fourteenth Amendment. Writing for the majority opinion in *Roe v. Wade*, Justice Blackmun noted that the right of privacy is "broad enough to encompass a woman's decision whether or not to terminate her pregnancy."[10]

It is important to understand that, although the decision did legalize abortion throughout the United States, it did not grant an *unlimited* right to abortion. In his decision, Blackmun noted that the states' "important interests in safeguarding health, maintaining medical standards, and protecting potential life" are strong enough that a state may regulate abortion "at some point in pregnancy."[11] The court added what has come to be known as its "trimester analysis": no government regulation during the first three months of pregnancy; limited regulation in the second trimester in order to protect women's health and safety; and the right of a state government to ban abortions during the third trimester, when the fetus is capable of living on its own.

That decision has proven to be one of the most controversial in the court's history. Many groups were pleased that the court had found that women did have a right to get an abortion, and many others were equally outraged. This latter group believed that abortion was murder, that the fetus was an individual from the moment of conception, and that no one had the right to take the life of an individual. Other critics of the decision disagreed with the court on different grounds. They believed the court had intruded on a sensitive issue that was best left to state governments to decide—state governments that were, in theory, the "voice of the people."

Since that decision was announced, the concept of abortion rights has become a dividing line in U.S. politics. There is a constant battle between those who believe in a woman's right to have an abortion (the "pro-choice" movement) and those who believe in protecting the lives of the unborn (the "pro-life" movement). As state legislatures have tested the limits of what is or is not acceptable government regulation of abortion, the lower courts often have had to decide if state laws on abortion are constitutional or unconstitutional. Many of these cases have worked their way up to the U.S. Supreme Court, which has the final say on the legality of all local, state, and federal laws.

Soon after the *Roe v. Wade* decision was announced, O'Connor, then still an Arizona state senator, voted against state proposals for regulations of abortion and against a resolution asking the U.S. Congress to prohibit abortion. On the other hand, she voted for legislation that restricted the use of state funds to help pay for abortions for poor women and voted for a bill that allowed hospital personnel to refuse to participate in abortions. In these votes, it is evident that O'Connor was trying to find a balance between those in favor of abortion and those who opposed it—a balance she would continue to seek when she herself became a U.S. Supreme Court justice. During her time on the Supreme Court, Sandra Day O'Connor would help decide many abortion cases.

MOVING ON
Even though she only had served in the state senate for a relatively short period of time, the work was taking its toll. Clashes between political parties and groups grew more heated, and O'Connor herself, known for her cool temper, began to let loose. A Republican senate committee chairman was furious that one of his bills had failed to reach the senate floor for a final vote. He told O'Connor, "If you were a man, I'd punch you in the mouth." Her response: "If you were a man, you could."[12]

Personal considerations were coming into play as well. Her boys were now teenagers and more demanding of her attention. She always had kept strict discipline with the boys, requiring them to rely on themselves and to do their part around the house. "My return to the job market necessitated that our three sons learn to be self-sufficient to a degree that would not have been true had I remained at home," she wrote years later. "They learned to cook and, when necessary, wash their clothes, and even to iron a shirt now and then."[13]

Still, as teenagers who occasionally got into trouble at school, they perhaps needed more personal attention than they had been getting. O'Connor's parents needed attention as well. They were aging, and Harry Day did not like his son Alan's efforts to modernize the way the ranch was being run. With all these issues coming into play, O'Connor announced in the spring of 1974 that she would not run for reelection. One month later, she made an additional announcement, one that would set her directly on the road to the Supreme Court.

Moving Up

On May 23, 1974, Sandra Day O'Connor announced that she was going to run for a new superior judgeship created by the Maricopa County Board of Supervisors. In her campaign literature, she wrote: "As a lawyer and as a legislator I am deeply concerned about the need to strengthen the enforcement of the laws that govern our conduct. As a citizen, a wife and a mother, I want to help replace fear in our streets with strength in our courtrooms."[1] After winning 70 percent of the vote in a primary battle with fellow Republican David Perry, she ran unopposed in the general election and took her seat on the bench in 1975.

She loved the work. She was her own boss, set her own schedule, and was able to interpret the law. "The whole experience of presiding over a trial in court is a remarkable experience," she told a reporter with the *Phoenix Gazette*. "You see every kind of human emotion and human value expressed and you see people in very tense situations and you listen . . . to some remarkable problems and situations of every kind."[2]

Many of the cases she heard were "ordinary," but even ordinary cases can have an extraordinary human element to them. In one such case, a businesswoman with two small children was charged with passing $3,500 worth of bad checks. The woman pled guilty and begged O'Connor not to give her a jail sentence that would separate her from her children. In making her decision, O'Connor said, "You have intelligence, beauty, and two small children. You come from a fine and respected family. . . . Someone with all your advantages should have known better."[3] O'Connor sentenced the woman to 5 to 10 years in prison. Back alone in her judge's chambers, O'Connor wept about the decision she had felt she needed to give.

She could be equally tough on the lawyers in her courtroom. "You didn't want to go in there if you weren't prepared, if you hadn't filed the papers when you were supposed to, if you hadn't researched your case properly, if you came in there on an argument without any authority and tried to snow her," said Alice Bendheim, a Phoenix attorney. "She did not appreciate having her time wasted."[4]

RUNNING FOR GOVERNOR?

Even while sitting on the bench, O'Connor remained part of the Republican Party establishment. In 1978, party leaders approached her about running for governor. O'Connor was reluctant, but the pressure continued. The party leaders felt that she had the best chance of any Republican to win the governorship.

O'Connor came close to saying yes, but then the new state Republican chairman, Jim Colter, announced that he was giving his support to another candidate. After Colter's announcement, O'Connor herself announced that she would not be a candidate. As her reason for not running, she explained that she wanted to spend more time with her family. By this time, however, two of her three sons were off at college. It seems more likely that she realized that without having the full backing of her party's leadership, the run would be more difficult than she wanted.

The Democratic Party candidate Bruce Babbitt defeated the man whom the Republican Party eventually nominated for governor, Evan Meacham. Babbitt, eager to prove that he was willing to work across party lines (and, some felt, just as eager to prevent O'Connor from running for governor against him in the future), appointed O'Connor to the Arizona Court of Appeals. Her work there would be far different from that as a trial judge.

Instead of working alone, she would be working in a three-person group. Instead of deciding questions of fact, she would be deciding broader questions of law and principle. Instead of conducting trials and listening to witnesses, she would be hearing oral arguments from lawyers for opposing sides presenting their views on the law that was being questioned. For example, in a murder case, a trial jury decides who actually committed the murder and the judge hands out the sentence. But a panel of appeals court judges decides on the differences, for example, between manslaughter and murder, or whether the defendant had been tried properly, or whether the evidence used against him or her was legal.

Indeed, most states have a three-tiered system of courts: trial, appeals (or appellate), and supreme. All of these courts have what is known as *general jurisdiction*, which means they can rule on virtually any kind of controversy that may arise. The federal court system also is made up of three tiers, with the U.S. Supreme Court at its top. Federal courts normally hear only cases that specifically involve federal laws or cases that deal with disputes between states or citizens of different states.

The federal courts also have the power to review and overturn state court decisions *if* they appear to go against the U.S. Constitution. This most often happens in criminal matters. For example, if a state court sentences a murderer to death, a federal court may review the case to make certain that the trial and sentencing were done according to the requirements of the Constitution.

O'Connor was sworn in as an appellate court judge on December 4, 1979. The week before this, she was invited by U.S. Supreme Court Justice Warren Burger to go to England with him as a U.S. representative at an Anglo-American legal conference in London. O'Connor had met Burger and impressed him on a vacation trip to Lake Powell, on the border of Utah and Arizona. Although she had less than five years on the bench, O'Connor was already making a name for herself within the nation's top legal circles. Just a year and a half later, she would be meeting with President Ronald Reagan to be interviewed to become the nation's first female Supreme Court justice.

TESTED

One day before making his announcement, President Reagan called O'Connor to tell her the news. " 'Sandra, I'd like to announce your nomination to the Court tomorrow,'" she later recalled him saying. In an interview with Joan Biskupic, O'Connor said she was "thunderstruck" by the president's call, and was concerned that her limited experience as a judge had not prepared her to sit on the nation's highest court. She was concerned also about becoming the first female justice: "It's fine to be the first, but you don't want to be the last."[5]

If O'Connor was unsure of what her reception would be, she needn't have been. "Justice Sandra Day O'Connor's place in history is already secure, based on the announcement that she will be President Reagan's nominee as the first woman on the United States Supreme Court," wrote B. Drummond Ayres Jr., in the *New York Times*.[6] Former Texas Congresswoman Barbara Jordan agreed: "I congratulate the President. The Supreme Court was the last bastion of the male: a stale dark room that needed to be cracked open. I don't know the lady, but if she's a good lawyer and believes in the Constitution, she'll be all right."[7]

While many praised her selection, some, such as the liberal magazine *The Nation*, questioned her qualifications for the position and wondered if she had been chosen only because she was a woman: "Despite the many kind words of her friends, Judge O'Connor's record is not even close to Supreme Court quality. She was not an exceptional lawyer or legal scholar, nor is she an outstanding judge."[8] Editorials such as these were few and far between. The press nearly unanimously approved of the selection, and the nominee found herself buried under letters from around the country, such as this one:

> I cannot begin to describe with what delight I viewed the surprising headlines in Chicago's newspapers the day of your nomination. I actually stood there with my mouth hanging open and an idiotic grin on my face, feeling overwhelmingly euphoric and proud.[9]

(Of course, not all the letters were positive. One writer even suggested to O'Connor that she get back into the kitchen and take care of her grandchildren and husband!)

CONFIRMATION

One group that had concerns about O'Connor being placed on the Supreme Court was the pro-life movement. Looking at her record on abortion in Arizona, members of this group were concerned that she was not anti-abortion enough, and that she would not be a voice against the *Roe v. Wade* decision. Her 1970 vote to decriminalize abortion came under review. The Rev. Jerry Falwell, a fierce anti-abortion advocate and leader of the group the Moral Majority, stated that he feared that O'Connor would support abortion on demand.

Many of these conservative opponents were silenced when leading conservative Senator Barry Goldwater spoke out in favor of his fellow Arizonian. Democrats, who might usually be found opposing a Reagan judicial selection, praised the president's selection as well. As supporters of the women's movement, Democrats were politically unable to vote against the first woman nominee for Supreme Court justice.

Despite what seemed likely to be an easy confirmation process, O'Connor took no chances. She spent much time preparing for the hearings, refreshing her memory about how she had voted and how her positions had evolved over the years, studying the records of the senators sitting on the Judiciary Committee, and asking others who had been through the process for advice. In the middle of July, O'Connor went to Washington for her first opportunity to meet the senators who would be voting on her nomination. In just seven days, O'Connor met with 39 senators, the Republican and Democratic leaders of the House of Representatives, and members of the American Bar Association. Not surprisingly, she charmed each and every one of them.

After that hurdle had been passed, O'Connor settled in to do her homework in earnest, going over briefing

Sandra Day O'Connor testifies at her judicial confirmation hearing in September 1981. O'Connor was overwhelmingly confirmed by the Senate 99–0 on September 21 and took her seat on the court on September 25.

books, discussing possible questions she would face, and getting suggestions on how to give her answers in the most politically acceptable way possible. For example, she was advised to stress her experience as a legislator and to let senators know that she personally found abortion morally objectionable. She underwent question-and-answer rehearsal sessions to prepare for the Judiciary Committee's hearings. But the night before the hearings began, she couldn't sleep, and she worried about "how [she] would be treated and how well [she] would be able to respond to the questions."[10]

She had no need to worry. She first made an opening statement that introduced her family and her philosophy of law: "My experience as a state court judge and as a state legislator has given me a greater appreciation of the important role the states play in our federal system. . . . Those experiences have strengthened my view that the proper role of the judiciary is one of interpreting and applying the law, not making it."[11] Then, she settled in to three days of questioning. On the first day she tried to give a clear explanation of her views on abortion:

> I have indicated to you . . . my own abhorrence of abortion as a remedy. It is a practice in which I would not have engaged, and I am not trying to criticize others in that process. There are many who have very different feelings on this issue. I recognize that, and I am sensitive to it. But my view is the product, I suppose, merely of my own upbringing and my religious training, my background, my sense of family values, and my sense of how I should lead my own life.[12]

It was a great answer. By linking her own background and family to her personal opposition to abortion, she reassured many of the pro-life movement that she would be an acceptable judge. And her recognition that others have different feelings on abortion gave hope to pro-choice advocates that she would not vote to overturn *Roe v. Wade*, should the opportunity arise. Finally, by refusing to say how she *might* decide on a case in the future, she allowed both groups to hope that she was on their side. As biographer Biskupic noted, "Activists on both sides read into her words what they wanted to hear."[13]

On September 21, 1981, the Senate voted 99 to 0 to confirm Sandra Day O'Connor. (One senator, Montana Democrat Max Baucus, supported O'Connor but was absent from the Senate at the time of the vote.) Even

Sandra Day O'Connor poses with her family and Chief Justice Warren Burger on the steps of the U.S. Supreme Court in Washington, D.C., in September 1981. This photo was taken prior to her swearing in as an associate justice of the Supreme Court. From left to right are: O'Connor's father, Harry Day; husband John J. O'Connor; mother Ada Mae Day; Sandra Day O'Connor; Warren Burger; and O'Connor's sons Brian, Jay, and Scott.

Jeremiah Denton, the fiercely anti-abortion senator from Alabama and the only member of the Judiciary Committee who voted against sending O'Connor's nomination to the full Senate, voted for her in the end. O'Connor, who had been awaiting the results of the vote in the offices of Senator Strom Thurmond, was thrilled and relieved when it was announced. On the steps of the Capitol, she addressed waiting reporters and tourists: "My hope is that ten years from now, after I've been across the street and worked for a while, they'll feel glad that they gave me this wonderful vote."[14]

THE PUBLIC SWEARING IN

Besides the private swearing-in of the new Supreme Court justice, there's a public ceremony, one filled with pomp and tradition. Richard Stengel of *Time* magazine described the ceremony for Justice O'Connor:

> O'Connor was escorted to the ornate marble-and-mahogany courtroom. While 500 invited guests looked on, she was seated in the chair once occupied by John Marshall, the Chief Justice (1801–1835) who introduced the principle of judicial review of executive and legislative acts, establishing the court's authority in the fledgling nation. The bailiff cried the traditional "oyez, oyez," and the eight Justices stood silently behind the wooden bench. O'Connor then took a second oath ("I do solemnly swear that I will support and defend the Constitution of the United States . . ."), and a clerk of the court helped Justice O'Connor slip on a black robe over her lavender-colored dress. With a quick smile and a sure step, O'Connor took her place beside her colleagues. . . . The robe was the same one she had worn while on the Arizona bench, and looked a bit tatty. "I'll buy a new one eventually," she promised. "They do get old, you know."*

*Richard Stengel, with Evan Thomas, "A New Order in the Court," *Time*. October 5, 1981. Available online at http://www.time.com/time/magazine/article/0,9171,921049-2,00.html.

What followed was a week of celebrations paying tribute to O'Connor's historic milestone. On September 25, 1981, she was sworn in at a private ceremony in the Supreme Court's conference room, attended by only President Reagan, First Lady Nancy Reagan, O'Connor's fellow members of the court, her husband and sons, and retiring justice Potter Stewart. O'Connor placed her right hand on two family Bibles held by her husband and repeated the judicial oath to "do equal right to the poor and to the rich."

Sandra Day O'Connor, 51 years old, had made history. She was now the first female justice in the history of the Supreme Court. O'Connor's place on the bench, based on who had been there the longest, was the chair next to her old friend, fellow associate justice William Rehnquist, at the far left of the court's chief justice, Warren Burger. Now would come the hard part. O'Connor would have to prove to the world that she deserved to be there.

New Woman
on the Court

All I knew was that the job would be a tremendous undertaking. I had no specific ideas about the mechanics of being a Justice, however, or what the decision-making process on the Court was really like. I hoped that I had the basic ability and could develop the skills not only to do the job but to do it well in order that not only women but most citizens would think that the President had made a good choice.[1]

—Sandra Day O'Connor

O'Connor's point is well taken. As discussed in the first chapter, the Supreme Court's workings are something of a mystery for most Americans, even ones with a legal background such as hers. Therefore, to understand Sandra Day O'Connor's career as a Supreme Court justice, it is necessary to understand just how the court itself operates.

THE WORKINGS OF THE COURT

The Supreme Court, as the nation's top court, is the final stop for any case that works its way through the nation's judicial system. But how exactly does the court receive its cases, and how does the court decide which cases it will hear?

Each year, the court receives more than 7,000 case applications through both the state and federal court systems. Of those 7,000 requests, the court accepts just a small percentage for full review and oral arguments—usually no more than about 100 cases for each year's term. About 100 additional cases are decided without oral arguments and full briefings.

It is the custom of the Supreme Court that at least four justices have to agree for the court to hear a case. Several important factors go into deciding which cases are heard and which ones are not. In O'Connor's words, the judges evaluate the importance of the issue before the court, the likelihood that it is an issue that will arise in other courts around the country, and whether courts around the country facing the same issue have reached conflicting decisions on it. If the case then warrants a hearing before the Supreme Court, the justices will accept it in order to try to establish a ruling that will apply to similar cases across the nation. Once the court decides which cases will be heard, the hard work begins. Each member of the court reads a summary of the information for each of the cases they will be hearing. This summary, called a brief, will prepare the members of the court for the next stage: oral arguments.

The court holds two-week oral argument sessions each month from October through April. Each side has a half-hour to present its argument. During that time justices often interrupt the attorney's argument to ask questions of their own. The person who brought the case to court goes first. This person is called the petitioner, and he or she may reserve time to answer the arguments of the opposing side, called the respondent, after that side has finished.

At the end of the oral arguments, the case is submitted for decision. The nine judges discuss the merits of the case and learn how each one thinks the case should be decided—and *why* they think it should be decided that way. Based on this discussion, the justices decide who will write the official opinion on the case. If the chief justice agrees with the side with the most votes, he has the right to assign the writing of the majority opinion to one of the other justices in the majority or can write the opinion himself. If the chief justice is not in the majority, the most senior justice in the majority makes the assignment. Sometimes the court decides to write an opinion for the minority—called a dissenting opinion, or a dissent. In a similar way to the majority opinion, if there is more than one justice on the minority side, it is the most senior justice joining the dissent who assigns the writing.

Here is where things get really interesting: Whichever justice writes the majority opinion, he or she must write it in such a way that his or her views agree with those of the other justices also voting in the majority. The first draft is then passed among the other justices voting in the majority. Each one has the option to sign it as is, to ask for revisions before signing, or to decide to write an opinion of his or her own, known as a concurring opinion. A concurring opinion suggests that, although that justice is voting with the majority, the justice has reasons why his or her vote in the majority differs from the other justices.

This process can be a long one, as draft after draft is written, with the writer hoping to get as many justices

JUDICIAL REVIEW

One of the more important powers of the U.S. Supreme Court is that of judicial review, which allows the judicial branch of the government to decide if governmental acts are constitutional. Through judicial review, judges demonstrate the rule of law by upholding the position of the Constitution over all branches of government. All courts in the United States, including federal, state, and local, have the power of judicial review, but it is the Supreme Court that has the final word.

Interestingly, the U.S. Constitution does not mention judicial review. In 1789, Congress passed the Judiciary Act, which gave federal courts the power of judicial review over acts of *state* government. It was not until 1803, when declaring an act of Congress unconstitutional in the case of *Marbury v. Madison*, that the Supreme Court extended its authority to declare acts of the *federal* government unconstitutional as well.

In his opinion, Chief Justice John Marshall justified the court's decision: "Certainly all those who have framed written constitutions contemplate them as forming the fundamental and paramount law of the nation, and consequently the theory of every such government must be, that an act of the legislature, repugnant to the Constitution, is void."* With those words, the model was set for the federal judicial branch to declare unconstitutional any acts of the federal government—either the legislative or executive branch—that violate the Constitution.

Marbury v. Madison (1803). Available online at http://encarta. msn.com/encyclopedia_761571106_2/marbury_v_madison.html.

as possible to sign off on his or her opinion. A majority opinion signed by each member of that majority has much more force as a legal opinion than does a majority vote with differing conclusions as to why that decision was reached. The Supreme Court's decisions are announced throughout the year, but mostly during the last months of the term—April, May, and June.

During the nine months the court is in session, the nine justices are extraordinarily busy. Oral arguments have to be heard, and time must be spent researching and thinking about the law, discussing the case with law clerks and other justices, and writing opinions.

STARTING OUT

Equipped with a staff of two secretaries and four law clerks, Justice O'Connor hit the ground running. On September 28, just three days after being sworn in, the justices' first meeting or "conference" was held to decide which cases would be heard in the upcoming session. Hundreds of appeals were waiting to be read, each one bearing the hopes of a petitioner aiming to get the Supreme Court to hear his or her case. O'Connor had a lot of work to catch up on.

She was prepared when the first conference was held in an oak-paneled room just off the chambers of the chief justice. As tradition dictated, O'Connor, as the newest justice, was given the seat closest to the door as the official "doorkeeper," letting people in and out and passing messages and requests for material to messengers waiting outside. As the newest justice, O'Connor had the job of taking notes on the meeting and giving them to the court clerk. It is somewhat ironic that the woman who turned down the position of legal secretary so many years earlier was now doing secretarial work as part of her new job as Supreme Court justice.

Here, the Supreme Court justices pose with President Reagan in the Supreme Court conference room on September 25, 1981. From left to right are: Justice Harry Blackmun, Justice Thurgood Marshall, Justice William Brennan, Chief Justice Warren Burger, President Ronald Reagan, Justice Sandra Day O'Connor, Justice Byron White, Justice Lewis F. Powell Jr., Justice William Rehnquist, and Justice John Paul Stevens.

It was here that she worked with the other eight justices for the first time. Chief Justice Warren Burger, a judicial conservative, believed that the Constitution was not a permit to solve social problems. William Brennan, then 75, had, in the words of Joan Biskupic, "a liberal vision of the Constitution as an evolving document that could be used to correct perceived social wrongs."[2] Byron White, then 64, held views that were becoming increasingly conservative. Thurgood Marshall, then 73, was the first

African-American justice and known as a tireless defender of individual rights. Harry Blackmun, at 70, had started out voting conservative but was moving more and more to the left. In fact, he was most famous for writing the majority opinion in the case of *Roe v. Wade*. There was also Lewis Powell, at 74, a Southern gentleman who was considered to be the court's voice of moderation. William Rehnquist, 57, O'Connor's long-time friend, was considered to be the court's most conservative member. And finally, there

JUSTICE THURGOOD MARSHALL

If Justice O'Connor spent her career battling sexist attitudes toward women in the workplace, Thurgood Marshall spent his career fighting to overturn the laws that had kept African Americans from enjoying their full rights as U.S. citizens.

Thurgood Marshall was born in Baltimore, Maryland, on July 2, 1908, the great-grandson of a slave. A graduate of Frederick Douglass High School in Baltimore and Lincoln University, he showed an early interest in the U.S. Constitution and in the law. He had wanted to apply to his hometown law school, the University of Maryland School of Law, but was told by the dean that he would not be accepted due to the school's segregation policy. (Years later, as a civil rights litigator, he successfully sued the school for this very policy in the case of *Murray v. Pearson*.)

Unable to attend the school of his choice, he went to law school at historically black Howard University, from which he graduated as valedictorian in 1933. He immediately went to work representing civil rights activists. He became a counsel for the National Association for the Advancement of Colored People was John Paul Stevens, 61, somewhat of a legal maverick, who was nonetheless building a reputation as a reliably liberal vote.

O'Connor quickly settled into the court's routines. She worked six days a week, often bringing home-cooked meals into the office on Saturdays for her clerks. For each case coming up before the court, O'Connor would read the background material, the briefs written by each of the parties in the case, memos written by her law clerks, and relevant

(NAACP), and over the next 23 years he won 29 of the 32 major cases he took for that organization, setting constitutional law models in such matters as voting rights and segregated transportation and education. Indeed, his crowning achievement came with *Brown v. Board of Education* (1954), which overturned the ruling in *Plessy v. Ferguson* (1896) that allowed "separate but equal" segregated institutions and facilities.

President John F. Kennedy named him to the U.S. Court of Appeals (1962–1965). President Lyndon Johnson first appointed him U.S. solicitor general (1965–1967) and then to the U.S. Supreme Court, where he became the first African American to serve as a Supreme Court justice. During his time on the court (1967–1991), he consistently voted with the court's liberal voting block as an advocate for the rights of minorities, women, children, and prisoners.

Forced by ill health to retire in 1991, he was replaced on the court by conservative justice Clarence Thomas. When Marshall died on January 24, 1993, he was hailed as an icon of the civil rights movement and a towering figure in U.S. history.

law review articles. "I think that most everything you do in life requires preparation," she said in an interview with the *Ladies' Home Journal*, "and if you are prepared and have thought about it, then things won't be a problem. If you feel you are not prepared . . . that's grounds for concern."[3]

As in law school, O'Connor was not afraid to jump in and ask questions, either at the judges' conference meetings or from the bench. She knew that her every move was being carefully watched by her fellow judges, the media, and the public at large. Being a trailblazer meant that she had to work harder than anyone else, but the results quickly paid off. In a letter written to his daughter in late October, Justice Powell wrote, "Justice O'Connor is off to an impressive start. It is quite evident that she is intellectually up to the work of the Court."[4]

As the term proceeded, O'Connor's approach soon became clear. As described by Joan Biskupic, the newest justice was firm on criminal defendants and led the arguments in favor of limiting the right of state prisoners to appeal to federal courts. And, not surprisingly, given her experience in the Arizona State Senate, she made the relationship between the federal government and state governments her "signature" concern.

For decades, the Supreme Court had given a larger role to the federal government in putting out regulations, at the expense of the rights of states to regulate themselves. In one of O'Connor's earliest opinions, a dissenting one, she wrote of the need to protect states from the federal government stepping in on state matters. By the end of her time on the Supreme Court, O'Connor's view on states' rights was no longer a dissenting view—it was the majority view.

ROSE V. LUNDY

One early case that caught her attention was the case of *Rose v. Lundy*. On paper, the case appeared to be not particularly interesting. It revolved around the basic legal principle of habeas corpus (literally translated as "you have the body"), which for legal purposes describes a written court order demanding that a government that is holding a prisoner to release him so that he can make his claims in court. Prisoners often seek habeas corpus to claim violations of their rights, such as the right to a lawyer, the guarantee against self-incrimination, or other rights guaranteed by the constitution.

In the case of *Rose v. Lundy*, Noah Lundy, a Tennessee man sentenced in state courts to 120 years in prison for various crimes, made several claims in federal court challenging his conviction. The problem was that some of Lundy's claims had never been argued in state court, something that was required before a prisoner turned to the federal courts. (This is known as a "mixed petition.") Despite this, a federal judge had decided to consider Lundy's claims, which resulted in an overturning of his convictions.

State officials in Tennessee appealed, arguing that all of Lundy's claims had to be fully examined in state court before they could be considered in federal court. The U.S. Court of Appeals for the Sixth Circuit, however, affirmed the earlier court's decision and allowed it to stand. The next step for Tennessee officials was the U.S. Supreme Court.

It was a closely watched case. State officials, who often felt bitter about federal courts jumping into what they saw as state matters, hoped that the court would reverse the decision. Prisoner rights advocates, on the other hand, knew that prisoners could file habeas corpus petitions themselves and often didn't fully understand which claims could be made in federal court and which could not. Advocates hoped that prisoners wouldn't be "punished" for a simple mistake.

In conference after hearing oral arguments, a majority of the Supreme Court voted in favor of the state of Tennessee against Lundy. Chief Justice Burger, voting in the majority, gave O'Connor the assignment of writing the opinion for the court. It was the first she had written. In it, she held that U.S. district court justices must dismiss mixed petitions without considering any of the claims. She wrote that prisoners took the risk of forfeiting a review of their claims if they had not been completely examined in state court, or if they first went ahead with their exhausted claims.

O'Connor had tried to reach a compromise position, not for the first time in her career. Two of the court's liberal justices, Blackmun and Brennan, both strongly dissented, with Blackmun stating that O'Connor's standards were a "trap for uneducated and indigent prisoners." Conservative justices such as Rehnquist felt that O'Connor didn't go far enough in restricting access to habeas corpus for state prisoners. Although she made some small changes (allowing Brennan, for example, to join some parts of her decision and to dissent with others), the basic outline of her opinion stood. State prisoners now found it more difficult to get their cases heard in federal court, and states' rights were strengthened by the decision.

ENMUND V. FLORIDA

This was one case in which Justice O'Connor thought that she had cobbled together a majority vote, but ultimately she lost it. Losing was not something she was accustomed to doing.

The case involved the death penalty and under what circumstances it could be applied constitutionally. On April 1, 1975, Sampson and Jeanette Armstrong came to the back door of the Florida farmhouse of Thomas and Eunice Kersey, falsely claiming they needed water for their overheated car. A robbery began, Eunice Kersey shot Jeanette Armstrong, and the Armstrongs ended up killing both Kerseys. Earl Enmund, the Armstrongs' accomplice, had been waiting in a parked car to help the Armstrongs escape. Enmund was convicted of murder and sentenced to the death penalty with the Armstrongs.

Enmund challenged his death penalty conviction. Since he did not kill or intend to kill the Armstrongs, his lawyers argued that the death penalty was cruel and unusual punishment, and as such, it was a violation of the Eighth Amendment to the Constitution. O'Connor thought that she had a majority to uphold Enmund's death penalty and began passing a copy of her opinion around to the other justices.

Joining her were justices Burger, Powell, and Rehnquist. O'Connor felt certain that she had the necessary fifth vote from Justice Blackmun, but he could not sign onto O'Connor's opinion, despite agreeing with it in large part. Instead, Blackmun decided to sign Justice White's opinion, which overturned Enmund's conviction. Blackmun wrote: "Although I continue to believe that the Eighth Amendment does not require in every case a finding of actual intent to kill before a capital sentence may be imposed . . . I agree with Justice White that the death penalty may not be inflicted where the defendant did not take life, did not attempt to take life, and did not intend to take life."[5]

In a letter to Justice Powell, who was rapidly becoming O'Connor's closest friend on the court, she said, "I am somewhat frustrated and quite concerned that my draft failed to attract a majority." But, she added, "In this business one must learn to 'grin and bear it.' "[6] It was still just her first term, and she was still somewhat new to the need to accept winning and losing and the ways of the court. There was still one large case remaining, though—one in which her vote would make all the difference.

Making Her Mark

The case was *Mississippi University for Women v. Hogan*. Again, the basics of the case were simple. Joe Hogan had been denied admission to a state-run nursing school that only admitted female students. Interest ran high as to how O'Connor would vote. Would she support the right of the state to keep its female-only school? Or would she agree that Hogan had been unconstitutionally discriminated against on the basis of his sex?

The state of Mississippi argued that the school was the first state-supported one for the higher education of women in the country and still fulfilled a need as an institution for women exclusively. For Hogan, it was a basic case of sexual discrimination. Wanting to improve his job prospects by earning a bachelor's degree in nursing, but unable and unwilling to move away from his hometown to go to school, he applied to the Mississippi University for Women for admission, but was turned down for the sole reason that he was a man.

Hogan took his case to court and lost before a U.S. district court judge before winning on appeal to the Fifth Circuit. That panel noted in its opinion that the state did not offer a similar single-sex educational program for men, and an exclusive women-only university was no longer needed as it had been in 1884. The panel ordered the school to admit Hogan, but the state appealed the decision. The case came before the Supreme Court on March 22, 1982.

Most women's rights groups were supporting Hogan in his suit and had filed a brief known as an *amicus curiae* on his behalf. ("Amicus curiae" means "friend of the court" and describes a person or organization that, although not a part of the suit, has a strong opinion about the case that they wish to establish in court.) The groups argued that even if the university's gender line had been created for the purpose of helping women, it might hurt others by feeding stereotypes of what makes up women's work. By stereotyping nursing as being only "women's work," the groups felt that the state was harming both women and men.

Two days after hearing arguments, the justices considered the case. Chief Justice Burger said that he would vote to reverse the lower-court decision and side with the university. Justice Brennan argued in favor of Hogan. If the school provided men and women with equal educational opportunities, its actions would have been permissible, he said; but since it did not, it was not.

Justice White agreed with Brennan, but he wanted to make sure that the decision did not go beyond just the nursing school and that it wouldn't set the policy for the entire university. Marshall, too, agreed to affirm the lower-court decision. Blackmun, while stating that he felt troubled by the school's founding mission of preparing women for traditional work, nonetheless voted for the university. He was concerned that by striking down the university's policy, every other state-run school through-out the country would have to go co-educational.

Justice Powell said that he wanted the university's policy to stand. He felt that there was a place for single-sex edu-cation, and that it benefited both sexes. Justice Rehnquist agreed with Powell, and then Stevens announced that he wanted to affirm the Fifth Circuit's decision for the same reasons Brennan did. That left the vote at a 4 to 4 tie, with just one vote waiting to be heard. Justice Sandra Day O'Connor had the deciding vote.

O'Connor, after much thought, decided to vote along with Justice Brennan. She voted to allow Hogan (or any other man) to get his nursing degree at the Mississippi University for Women. It was clear to her that Hogan had been discriminated against solely on the basis of his sex. By a 5 to 4 decision, the Supreme Court decided that the nation's oldest public school for women had to accept men.

Now it was up to Justice Brennan, as the senior justice in the majority, to decide who was going to write the opinion. After a week's thought, he decided that O'Connor was the best person for the job for two reasons: The opinion would have more significance coming from the only woman on the court and, if he assigned the decision to one of the more lib-eral justices voting in the majority, there was the possibility they might go further in their opinion than O'Connor was prepared to go, and therefore lose her vote.

More than a month later, the court opinion was made public. On July 1, O'Connor said that the Constitution does not allow a state-run school to provide a special educa-tion for one sex without providing an equal education for the other. She noted that by excluding males from nursing school, the university tended "to perpetuate the stereotyped view of nursing as an exclusively women's job."[1] The woman who had fought sexual stereotypes her entire career had taken a strong stand in favor of equal opportunities for *both* sexes.

As O'Connor's biographer Joan Biskupic put it, "The Mississippi case helped define O'Connor. Equal rights between the sexes was a subject that had long engaged her, and she crafted an opinion that she believed made a difference in American life."[2] At the end of her first term, O'Connor not only had written an opinion on a subject of major importance to her, she had shown an ability to steer a path between rigid conservatism and liberalism.

LIFE AS A JUSTICE

Not only was she settling into life on the bench, she was settling into life in Washington, D.C. as well, entertaining and socializing as she always had done in Arizona. Even her offices in the Supreme Court building reflected her Arizona heritage: Navajo rugs and Western art from the Heard Museum in Phoenix, ceramics by Southwestern artists, and Native American crafts from the Lazy B. All these things found places of honor on walls, desks, and tables. John O'Connor was settling into his new life, too, joining the Washington law firm of Miller and Chevalier, while finding time to play golf with new friends President Ronald Reagan, Attorney General William French Smith, and Secretary of State Alexander Haig.

But misfortune can have a way of intruding in even the happiest of times. For some time, O'Connor's parents' health had been worsening. Ada Mae was suffering from Alzheimer's disease. Harry Day, always the strong and tireless rancher, was now so ill from emphysema that he needed an oxygen tank near him at all times.

On April 10, 1984, Harry Day died from emphysema-related heart disease. O'Connor learned of her father's death from her brother, Alan. Although the news was upsetting, it wasn't totally unexpected. O'Connor took charge of the funeral arrangements and had a simple memorial service at the ranch, as her father had requested. O'Connor, her sister, and her brother each spoke, and their father's ashes were taken to the top of Round Mountain.

THE COURT MOVES RIGHT

The Supreme Court, which tended to be liberal through-out the 1960s and 1970s, was becoming more conservative. Several of the liberal members of the court, such as Blackmun and Brennan, in part blamed O'Connor for this swing. Even *Time* magazine, in examining her first years on the court, called her Rehnquist's "Arizona Twin,"[3] because she so often voted with her conservative colleagues. Indeed, relations between Blackmun and O'Connor remained tense due to O'Connor's tendency to join with the growing conservative majority.

At the same time, O'Connor sought to separate herself from the conservatives and to find a middle ground between the two camps. Biskupic wrote:

DID YOU KNOW?

Sandra Day O'Connor is an avid golfer. She began playing in her forties, learning with a pro and hitting bucket after bucket of balls for more than two years before she was happy enough with her game to play with other people. In the year 2000, at the age of 70, she finally hit her first hole-in-one, and her shout of pure delight was heard across the greens.

It was during this period that O'Connor showed herself—at least to some insiders—to be a shrewd player. She ran ideas by Powell and worked with him to obtain a majority. She made a practice of showing drafts of her opinions to other select justices to solicit interest, protect a vote she did not want to lose, or prompt a justice to be ready to circulate a memo of approval when she gave her draft opinion to them all. She kept tabs on a vacillating [undecided] justice who might be a fifth vote for a position she favored.[4]

The ability to bring people together, to build a union, and to compromise in order to get something done—the skills that she had learned as a state senator were among the great abilities that O'Connor brought to the Supreme Court.

Of course, O'Connor wasn't working alone. She had her team of law clerks to assist her. She was thought of as a tough but fair boss, someone who demanded the best from her clerks. At the same time, she kept an interest in their personal lives and, on occasion, took them out on "field trips" to keep them entertained and amused. She also organized aerobics classes for her female law clerks, and it was clear that their attendance was expected.

CHANGES ON THE COURT

In the case of *Garcia v. San Antonio Metropolitan Transit Authority*, the Supreme Court had to decide whether federal minimum wage and overtime standards could be forced on state and local governments.[5] When the case was first heard in 1983, O'Connor joined justices Burger, Blackmun, Powell, and Rehnquist in saying that the federal government could not force federal wage standards on cities. However, as months passed while the opinion-writing process went on, Justice Blackmun decided to change his vote. Now

Supreme Court Justice Sandra Day O'Connor is photographed in her chambers at the Supreme Court on June 25, 2002. By the mid-1980s, O'Connor was seen as the court's crucial swing vote.

the majority vote said that federal wage standards *could* be forced on cities.

The four dissenting justices were perplexed at Blackmun's change of heart and attempted to postpone the court's decision. They hoped that over the summer there might be a change in the court's membership and, with it, a change in vote. But no such luck. When the decision was announced in 1985, O'Connor found herself on the losing side.

As Biskupic points out, the San Antonio case was proof that one justice on a closely divided court could change the law. More and more, O'Connor came to realize the importance of being in the center, of being the swing judge who could influence the laws of an entire nation with one vote.

As the court's term drew to an end in June 1986, the line-up of the court was about to change as well. Chief Justice Warren Burger announced his intention to resign. President Reagan quickly announced that he was going to promote Justice Rehnquist from associate justice to chief

SANDRA DAY O'CONNOR AND JOHN RIGGINS

O'Connor gained headlines for an incident that happened outside the court in 1985. It occurred at the Washington Press Club's Salute to Congress dinner, where her dining partner, the Washington Redskins' famed running back John Riggins, had apparently had too much to drink. Turning to her, he said, "Come on, Sandy baby, loosen up. You're too tight."* Riggins ended the evening asleep on the floor, with waiters gingerly stepping over him as they served dessert.

The next day, the embarrassed Riggins sent O'Connor a dozen roses to apologize, but the Arizona cowgirl, used to the occasional drunken ranch hand, was more amused by the incident than anything else. Within weeks, O'Connor and the other women in her aerobics class could be seen wearing T-shirts that said "Loosen up at the Supreme Court." Years later, when Riggins made his acting debut at a local Washington theater, O'Connor was there in person to present him with a dozen roses at his curtain call.

---

* Elizabeth Kastor, "John Riggins' Big Sleep: He Came, He Jawed, He Conked Out," *Washington Post*, February 1, 1985.

justice. Taking Rehnquist's place on the bench would be Antonin Scalia, the first Italian American to sit on the Supreme Court, and a favorite of conservatives nationwide. With that decision, Reagan was inching closer to a dream Republicans had held for the previous 20 years: a conservative majority on the court.

Then, in 1987, Justice Lewis Powell announced his decision to resign. O'Connor was heartbroken. Powell had been a friend, mentor, and valued colleague since she joined the court. As a replacement, President Reagan's first choice, Robert Bork, proved to be too controversial and conservative for many members of the U.S. Senate. He was rejected by a vote of 58 to 42.

Reagan then nominated U.S. Appeals Court Judge Douglas Ginsburg. His name had to be withdrawn just 10 days later when it became public that he had smoked marijuana while a professor at Harvard Law School. For his third attempt, Reagan played it safe, picking U.S. Court of Appeals Judge Anthony Kennedy. Judge Kennedy was approved by a unanimous vote of the U.S. Senate.

The upcoming 1988 to 1989 court session looked to be an interesting one. Already on the calendar were cases involving the use of racial preferences, rules for sex-discrimination lawsuits, the use of the death penalty on the mentally disabled and for defendants who had committed crimes before the age of 18, as well as an important case involving abortion rights. It would be a particularly busy and important nine months.

But just two weeks after the court's opening session, O'Connor was given devastating news that would change her perspective on life forever.

Finding a
Middle Ground

The diagnosis was breast cancer. O'Connor, always so physically active and healthy, was staggered. "I couldn't believe I was hearing this," she told the National Coalition for Cancer Survivorship. "It couldn't be true. I'm too busy. I feel fine. You can't be serious."[1]

Unfortunately, it was true. Doctors told her that there was no time to waste: The cancerous breast would have to be removed immediately. Two weeks after receiving the news, O'Connor entered Georgetown University Hospital for surgery and chemotherapy. Those two weeks, O'Connor later told close friends, were the worst of her life.

As usual, though, O'Connor faced her disease not as a tragedy but as a challenge. And characteristically, the night before entering the hospital, she kept a promise to give a speech at Washington and Lee Hospital. Immediately after her operation, she released a statement to the public in her classic no-nonsense style. "I underwent surgery for breast cancer. It was found to exist in a very early form and stage. The prognosis is for total recovery. I do not anticipate missing any oral arguments."[2] She left the hospital on October 26, allowing herself just five days to recover before returning to court for a two-week round of oral arguments. True to her word, she missed no arguments and maintained her full workload throughout the 1988 to 1989 term.

Although exhausted by surgery and chemotherapy, O'Connor was relieved to have her work to fall back on, to have "a job that was hard and important."[3] She asked for no favors at work, no special treatment. Always her father's daughter, she did what she had to do. Indeed, within weeks of leaving the hospital, she also was back to her usual rounds of social engagements. There was no way that she was going to allow herself to be beaten by her disease or treatment.

What the disease did do, however, was to give her a new sense of the shortness of life. Speaking about her experience in 1994, O'Connor told an audience: "Having this disease made me more aware than ever before of the transitory nature of life here on Earth, of my own life. And it made me value each and every day of life more than ever before."[4] It would be left to observers to see how this experience might possibly change her stance on the court as well.

NEW CASES, NEW CHALLENGES

As 1989 began, the United States had a new president, George H.W. Bush, and the Supreme Court had new cases before it that were certain to stir up argument and controversy both inside and outside the court. One of those cases was *Teague v. Lane*. Frank Teague was an Illinois resident who was convicted in 1980 of armed robbery and the attempted murder of police officers. Teague, who was African American, claimed that he had not received a fair trial because he had been tried by an all-white jury.

Each side in a case always has been able to use a set number of so-called "challenges" to screen potential jurors. A potential juror can be struck from a case if he or she is determined to be unable to judge the case fairly; this is called an "exemption for cause." Another way to strike a juror from a case is with a "peremptory exemption," which may be made for any reason without the need for explanation. The Supreme Court had ruled previously that peremptory exemptions could not be made for reasons of race. However, in the *Teague* case, the prosecutor had used his right to challenge prospective jurors and had struck down prospective jurors who were African American.

In his suit, Teague claimed that the exclusion of African Americans from his jury was a violation of his Sixth Amendment right to be judged by a jury that was a fair representation of his community. O'Connor, as a former state-court judge, felt that the case should not even be heard by the Supreme Court. She believed that prisoners convicted by the states often went too far in defying state-court rulings by appealing to the federal courts. After conference, it was clear that a majority of the justices agreed with O'Connor that Teague was barred from having the federal courts interfere with the state court's decision on his case.

Problems arose, however, when O'Connor began to pass around an early copy of her opinion, which severely limited the right of federal judges to hear prisoners' petitions. Indeed, she went one step further by insisting that prisoners, when making their appeals to the federal courts, could only rely on the laws that had been in place when their convictions became final. They could *not* rely on any changes in the rule of law that may have come out of a later Supreme Court decision.

The results of this opinion were far-reaching. The law is constantly changing, and the liberal wing of the court felt it was unreasonable for prisoners to "lose out" simply because certain rights weren't legally recognized at the time of their convictions. O'Connor, however, was able to put together a majority for her approach. She had won a major battle and had taken the case and its meanings far beyond what anyone had imagined when the court first agreed to hear the case. Once again, the one-time state senator and state judge had struck a blow to the rights of federal courts over state courts.

Personal problems also arose for O'Connor in the spring of 1989. On March 3, Ada Mae Day, O'Connor's 85-year-old mother, died. Then, O'Connor learned that the *Washington Post* was planning on publishing a story that claimed a slip-up in judicial ethics on her part. In 1988, O'Connor had written a letter to an Arizona Republican activist, which was later used by the state Republican Party to boost support for a party resolution declaring that the United States was "a Christian nation . . . based on the absolute law of the Bible."[5] Protests immediately erupted from both Jewish leaders and civil libertarians. O'Connor found herself criticized by attorneys on both the right and left sides of the political spectrum. (She later said that she was sorry it had been used for political purposes.)

While O'Connor was the center of media attention because of that letter, it was becoming increasingly clear to court observers that O'Connor had become the center of the court. It was often her vote that controlled which direction the court would move. *American Lawyer* magazine said in June 1989 that,

> . . . for now, at least, she is the one who determines which side wins the biggest 5-to-4 decisions and

how broadly they are written. . . . She is the most moderate member of the new conservative majority, the closest thing we have, for better or worse, to a living oracle of the evolving Constitution. To divine the direction of the law, watch what she does.[6]

Controversial decisions continued throughout the 1988 to 1989 term. One decision struck down a public nativity scene on the staircase of the Allegheny County Courthouse, for appearing to be an endorsement of a particular religion. However, the Supreme Court did find it permissible to display an 18-foot (5.5 m) Hanukkah menorah alongside a 45-foot (14 m) Christmas tree outside Pittsburgh's city-county building, with O'Connor arguing that the display offered "a message of pluralism and freedom of belief."[7]

Late June saw O'Connor writing the majority rulings for two important cases involving the death penalty. In the case of *Penry v. Lynaugh*, O'Connor declared in her opinion that despite the fact that the Constitution banned cruel and unusual punishment, that ban did not prohibit a state from executing a mentally disabled convict who had been declared able to stand trial. Similarly, in the case of *Stanford v. Kentucky*, O'Connor held that the Constitution did not bar the execution of a defendant who was only 16 years old when he committed his crime.

In both cases, O'Connor's argument moved along the same line: that the nation as a whole had not spoken out against the executions of the mentally disabled and of children. She made it clear that she believed that the surest indicator of modern values in such cases was in legislation enacted by state legislatures. And, for example, since only one state with the death penalty had banned the execution of mentally disabled persons, a national agreement had not yet been reached.

WEBSTER V. REPRODUCTIVE HEALTH SERVICES

There was one final case to be decided in the 1988 to 1989 term: *Webster v. Reproductive Health Services*. This case would be a test of whether *Roe v. Wade* would remain the law of the land. How would Sandra Day O'Connor vote? What, in fact, was her stance on abortion?

In earlier Supreme Court decisions, O'Connor had sided with the states in their right to regulate abortion. But that was years earlier, when Justice Blackmun still had a five-vote majority solidly in favor of upholding *Roe v. Wade*. The balance of the court had shifted since that time, and it seemed possible that a majority of justices might move in the other direction. As was usually the case, it appeared that Sandra Day O'Connor would hold the deciding vote.

The preamble to a 1986 Missouri law declared that "the life of each human being begins at conception," notes Biskupic. The law barred using public funds for counseling about abortion and prohibited public hospitals and public employees from performing abortions if they were not necessary to save the mother's life. Additionally, if a woman who wanted an abortion was at least 20 weeks pregnant, physicians were required to test to see if the fetus was able

IN HER OWN WORDS

Sandra Day O'Connor believes in putting her best effort into everything she does. She once said:

> Do the best you can in every task, no matter how unimportant it may seem at the time. No one learns more about a problem than the person at the bottom.

to live outside of the mother's womb. This section appeared to be in direct contradiction with one of the basic parts of the *Roe v. Wade* decision, which said that the state could *only* regulate abortions during the second trimester (roughly 13 to 24 weeks) in order to protect the health of the mother. Would the court allow the Missouri law to stand? Would the conservatives on the court be able to use the case as an opportunity to overturn *Roe v. Wade*?

Oral arguments regarding the case were held on April 26, 1989. Tensions were high within the court, as both sides presented their case. The justices asked many questions, with O'Connor and Kennedy leading the way. To many observers, it seemed obvious that those two justices had not yet made up their minds, and the direction of the court would be in their hands.

Two days later, in their private conference, the nine justices cast their votes and made their opinions known. Chief Justice Rehnquist went first, as was customary. He said that he would uphold all of the Missouri regulations, and he made it clear that he wanted to overturn *Roe* and let each state decide the matter. However, as he was unsure of how far O'Connor was willing to go, he suggested modifying the basis of *Roe* without overturning it altogether.

Justice Brennan, 83 at the time, was next. As expected, he argued that *Roe* had been decided correctly and that the Missouri laws should be overturned. Justice White wanted to uphold the Missouri regulations, and once again he voiced his belief that there was no constitutional right to abortion. Justice Marshall voted to affirm the lower court's overturning of the Missouri laws. Blackmun agreed, as did Stevens.

Next up was O'Connor. She said that the tests to determine whether a fetus could live on its own should be allowed, along with the restrictions on state medical personnel. What remained uncertain was whether or not she would vote to overturn *Roe*. Stating that she did not want to go any further than she had in previous cases when she voted *for* state regulations, she still gave hope to the conservative block that she might, at the very least, vote to severely restrict *Roe*.

Scalia declared that he wanted to use the case to overturn *Roe*. Last up was the court's newest justice, Anthony Kennedy. Justice Kennedy felt that issues such as abortion should be up to the voters in individual states to decide. This left some thinking that Kennedy, too, would vote to overturn *Roe*.

With all the votes counted, Chief Justice Rehnquist had the five votes necessary to at least overturn the lower court's decision and put the Missouri law back in place. What was still uncertain, however, was how far the court's decision would go. It was also uncertain whether or not Rehnquist would be able to persuade O'Connor to sign on to an opinion that severely restricted abortion rights.

O'Connor's oldest son Scott and his wife were expecting their first child in five months. Would that influence her decision? O'Connor herself had just received good news that tests for recurrence of cancer were negative and the outlook for total recovery was excellent. Would that in some way influence her decision? Some female law clerks working for other justices, concerned about which way O'Connor might vote, even considered having one clerk pretend that she was pregnant to illustrate for O'Connor the difficulties that a pregnant woman might have. The idea was quickly dismissed.

Rehnquist passed around his draft opinion upholding the Missouri regulations and presenting a new legal standard that would allow abortion restrictions if they "reasonably further the state's interest in protecting potential human life." O'Connor made it clear that she could not sign on.

Instead, while voting to uphold the Missouri regulations, she made it clear in her opinion that not only was she not going to overturn *Roe v. Wade*, but that she was "backing away from the critical statements about *Roe* she had made in earlier cases."[8] After discussing her reasons for allowing the Missouri law to stand—which she insisted did not go against the *Roe* decision—she stated her reasons for not signing on to Rehnquist's opinion. "When the constitutional invalidity of a State's abortion statute actually turns on the constitutional validity of *Roe v. Wade* [which O'Connor believed the Missouri case did not], there will be time enough to reexamine *Roe*. And to do so carefully."[9]

The justices who wanted to overturn *Roe* were furious. Justice Scalia said bluntly in his concurring statement to Rehnquist's opinion: "Justice O'Connor's assertion that a 'fundamental rule of judicial restraint' requires us to avoid reconsidering *Roe* cannot be taken seriously." On the other hand, Justice Blackmun, writing in a dissent joined by Brennan, Marshall, and Stevens, gave a sigh of relief: "For today, at least, the law of abortion stands. . . . For today, the women of this nation still retain the liberty to control their destinies."[10]

O'Connor had again steered a cautious middle ground. While upholding the right of Missouri to regulate abortion within reason, she also made it clear that she had no intention of voting to overturn *Roe v. Wade*. Conservative commentators were furious at what seemed a betrayal of conservative principles, but O'Connor stood her ground. After all, there were more cases to decide, including another involving abortion rights.

That other case was *Hodgson v. Minnesota*, involving a Minnesota statute that required a physician to notify both biological parents of an underage teen at least 48 hours before performing an abortion on her. There was a fallback position included in the law, should the Supreme Court find the statute unconstitutional (states often enact laws with the idea in mind of testing how far the Supreme Court

Pro- and anti-abortion demonstrators hold up signs on the steps of the Supreme Court building in Washington, D.C., on July 3, 1989. The protests came after the court ruled on the Missouri abortion case, which gave states greater power to limit abortion.

will let them go): The minor would be allowed to go to a judge and present her case to explain why she was unable to get permission from her parents.

Jane Hodgson, a physician and reproductive-rights activist, challenged the law, arguing that it interfered with a teenager's right to an abortion. This was especially the case when the underage girl came from a divorced or dysfunctional family. Hodgson also suggested that a young girl approaching a judge was not an easy alternative. What teenage girl would feel comfortable trying to convince a judge to allow her to get an abortion?

Once again, the Supreme Court was closely divided. Chief Justice Rehnquist, along with justices Scalia, White, and Kennedy, wanted to uphold the Minnesota law. Justices Blackmun, Stevens, Brennan, and Marshall all wanted to strike down the law. Both sides were making whatever arguments they could to win O'Connor's tie-breaking vote.

Throughout her career as a judge, O'Connor had supported the rights of individual states to regulate abortion. But this case was different. Perhaps because she was a woman, she was able to see the difficulty that a pregnant teenager might face, living in an abusive family and having to tell both parents that she was getting an abortion. Justice Stevens, according to Joan Biskupic, was quickly becoming the go-between for O'Connor and the liberal justices. He went to work on O'Connor, trying to win her over to join a decision overturning the Minnesota law.

It worked. Stevens was able to put together an opinion that all four liberal judges and O'Connor could sign. O'Connor agreed that the Minnesota law was unconstitutional, writing, "[T]he primary constitutional deficiency lies in [the statute's] imposition of an absolute limitation on the minor's right to obtain an abortion."[11] It was the first time that O'Connor had ever ruled against a state's abortion regulation.

AN EVER-GROWING INFLUENCE

O'Connor, now at the center of the court, was perhaps its most influential member. In any closely divided case, her vote often changed the balance. As even long-time members such as Justice Brennan came to realize, they would have to position their opinions toward the center in order to win O'Connor's vote.

After just nine years on the court, O'Connor had learned how to line up votes as effectively as Justice Brennan, a

34-year veteran. As Biskupic points out, by 1990, O'Connor generally had more votes with which to start building her majority, compared to Brennan. The change in the balance of power was particularly clear in criminal cases, where O'Connor was consistently able to put together a majority to restrict the rights of the accused and of prisoners.

One such case was that of *Coleman v. Thompson*. Roger Keith Coleman was a Virginia coal miner who had been convicted of raping and murdering his sister-in-law. Coleman continuously proclaimed his innocence—pointing out that even though his clothes were covered with coal dust on the day of the killing, there was no coal dust found in the victim's home. He challenged the fairness of his murder trial and claimed that he had been denied effective counsel because his court-appointed lawyers had never handled such a major case.

The Supreme Court ruled that Coleman did not have the right to present his claim in federal court. Coleman's lawyer had been late in filing his state habeas corpus appeal, missing the Virginia deadline by just three days. Because of this, his case was not heard in state court, as was mandatory before turning to the federal system. For Justice O'Connor,

DID YOU KNOW?

Sandra Day O'Connor was featured in a documentary about a group of painters. In October 2006, O'Connor sat down to have her portrait painted by 25 artists, both amateur and professional, who meet and work together weekly in New York City. The 25 portraits were shown at the National Portrait Gallery in Washington, D.C., and the documentary about the process, "Portraits of a Lady," has been shown on HBO.

the case was simple. When possible, the state should be trusted to do the right thing without federal interference. The influence of her father, who held lifelong skepticism about the power of the federal government, remained strong. "[The case] concerns the respect that federal courts owe the states and the states' procedural rules when reviewing the claims of state prisoners in federal habeas corpus,"[12] O'Connor wrote. She went on to insist that the Virginia courts were fair in punishing Coleman for his lawyer's mistake in missing the deadline.

Dissenters on the court were outraged, claiming that O'Connor and the rest of the majority were more concerned about "procedures" than they were with Coleman's guilt or innocence. The editorial page of the *New York Times* added to the criticism: "In the name of states' rights, the Court has produced a terrible injustice. . . . Is it fair to penalize the prisoner for his lawyer's mistake? Certainly, says Justice Sandra Day O'Connor for the majority."[13]

Roger Coleman was executed by the state of Virginia on May 20, 1992, swearing his innocence until the end. In 2006, Virginia governor Mark Warner ordered Coleman's DNA testing to be redone. When the test results came back, they confirmed Coleman's guilt.

O'Connor's influence was about to become even stronger. On July 20, 1990, Associate Justice William Brennan, 84 years old and in poor health, announced that he was resigning. In his 30-year history on the court, he had, according to both critics and supporters, "more of an effect on the law than anyone else in the last half century."[14] He had supported civil liberties, the rights of the individual, the freedom of the press, and the power of the federal government to direct the states. Yet, with the appointment of O'Connor to the bench, his influence had been gradually fading, and now he was gone. Sandra Day O'Connor was now the most influential justice on the Supreme Court.

The Most Powerful Woman in the Nation

She had lost her father. She had lost her mother. Then, in 1993, the nearly unthinkable happened. With her brother becoming too old to run the ranch properly, and with none of her children or her brother's children prepared to take on the work, the decision was made to sell the Lazy B. It was a difficult time for her: Of all the Day children, she had been the most reluctant to give it up.

Still, as was always the case in her life, O'Connor was ready to put the loss behind her and move on. She had a life to live and a job to do, and she was as determined as ever to do her best.

The court's newest justice was David Souter, who had spent seven years on the New Hampshire Supreme Court and three months on the U.S. Court of Appeals for the

First Circuit before being selected by President George H.W. Bush. Little was known about his judicial philosophy. Republicans assumed that he would be a solid conservative choice. That prediction turned out to be mistaken, to say the least.

O'Connor, as was her style, did her best to help introduce the bachelor justice to life in Washington. She invited him home for Thanksgiving, introduced him to women, and made him a part of her social circle. At first, Souter voted along with the court's conservative wing, but gradually he moved further and further to the left, much to the dismay of the Republicans who had voted for him in the first place.

Souter would soon be joined by another new justice. Thurgood Marshall announced his resignation on June 27, 1991. His replacement would be Clarence Thomas, a 43-year-old African-American judge on the U.S. Court of Appeals for the District of Columbia Circuit. Thomas was as conservative in his judicial philosophy as Marshall was liberal.

Unlike the hearings for David Souter, which went smoothly, Thomas's were instantly infamous for the amount of anger and conflict they aroused. Many felt that it was an insult to replace Marshall with a judge so unlike him in so many ways. Charges of sexual harassment raised their ugly head; but in the end, Thomas was approved by a 52 to 48 vote. It was the closest vote for a Supreme Court justice in more than 100 years.

Thomas would prove to be a reliably conservative vote. Although he and O'Connor did not always agree, as Joan Biskupic pointed out, "the addition of Justice Thomas gave O'Connor a new advantage. His vote allowed her to turn some of her most vigorous dissents into majority opinions."[1] In criminal rights cases and cases regarding voting rights, O'Connor remained the determining fifth vote.

THE WAR OVER ABORTION CONTINUES

In 1992, the new court line-up took on its most important abortion case since *Webster*. It was a case that once again had the potential to allow the court to overturn *Roe v. Wade*.

The case was *Planned Parenthood of Southeastern Pennsylvania v. Casey*. Pennsylvania law required that a married woman could not get an abortion without first informing her husband of her intentions. It also placed a 24-hour waiting period on a woman before she could actually get the procedure and required the woman's physician to give her a complete tutorial on fetal development and the abortion procedure, so that the woman would be able to give "informed consent."

A district court judge had declared the law void, but the U.S. Court of Appeals for the Third Circuit later restored it by relying largely on a narrow interpretation of O'Connor's own 1989 opinion in the case of *Webster*. Once again, a state was testing the boundaries of what was allowed under *Roe v. Wade*. Once again, observers on all sides of the question anxiously awaited the court's decision. Would this be the case that overturned *Roe v. Wade*?

After asking many questions during oral arguments, the justices settled in at the conference table two days later. Chief Rehnquist had put together a majority that would uphold all of the Pennsylvania provisions, with the exception of the one requiring a woman to notify her husband: Why, after all, should the wife be required to inform her husband about something that was legally her choice alone? The problem that Rehnquist faced was how far he would be able to go in his opinion to restrict *Roe v. Wade*.

O'Connor and Souter said they would not go so far as to say that the 1973 court had been wrong in finding a "fundamental right" to abortion. On this vote, the pivot turned out to be Justice Kennedy. He had previously come out against *Roe* and had even signed off on Rehnquist's dissenting opinion in the 1989 *Webster* case. Since then, however, his opinion had changed. He had come to accept that a decision to have an abortion was a personal choice protected by the Constitution's guarantee of privacy.

The trio of O'Connor, Souter, and Kennedy set out to work on an opinion that would basically affirm *Roe v. Wade* while throwing out the questions on trimester. They would instead establish a standard that would prohibit any restrictions that placed an "undue burden" on a woman wishing to end her pregnancy. In addition, they sought to explain, once and for all, to the American people exactly why *Roe* should endure.

Upon completing their draft, the three began circulating their opinion. They took suggestions from Justice Stevens on reordering the sections so that the affirmation of *Roe* came first, which would allow him and Justice Blackmun to sign off on it. With that, their opinion was completed. Although the court upheld the majority of the Pennsylvania law, *Roe v. Wade* was still safe. In their opinion, the trio made clear one reason *why* they wanted to uphold *Roe*: For nearly 20 years, they held, men and women had been in relationships and had made choices trusting that *Roe v. Wade* would maintain the right to an abortion. To those three judges, it would be unfair to remove that certainty.

Although the right to abortion was safe for the time being, its existence was still hanging on by a thread. With the change of just one vote, *Roe v. Wade* could have been overturned. Although those on the far left and far right found themselves unsatisfied with the decision, the majority of Americans approved of O'Connor's "middle way" on abortion rights. It allowed for some restrictions on abortion while at the same time maintaining its legality.

A NEW FRIENDSHIP, A NEW RIVALRY

In 1993, Justice Byron White announced his retirement. President Bill Clinton, a Democrat, jumped at the opportunity to place the first new liberal justice on the court in over 20 years. He turned to Ruth Bader Ginsburg, a former legal advocate for women's rights and a member of the U.S. Court of Appeals for the District of Columbia. Ginsburg already had successfully argued five cases before the Supreme Court. After the Senate confirmed Ginsburg by a vote of 96 to 3, Sandra Day O'Connor was no longer the sole woman on the court.

Although the two female justices on the Supreme Court rarely saw eye to eye on matters of law, they quickly became good friends. O'Connor, as she had done with each new justice, did her best to help Ginsburg fit in to her new position. "Justice O'Connor is the most helpful big sister anyone could have,"[2] Ginsburg remarked.

O'Connor could use all the friends she could get. With her new position of prominence on the Supreme Court, she increasingly became a target of both praise and criticism. In the *Los Angeles Times Magazine*, Howard Kohn wrote that, due to her influence, O'Connor was, "arguably, the most powerful woman in the nation."[3] Others, however, were not nearly so kind. Many legal scholars, for example, disapproved of her cautious step-by-step approach to the law. Because she refused to take bold stances, her critics felt her decisions lacked clarity and made it difficult for lower court judges to apply her decisions to similar cases in their own courts. One of her harshest critics, in fact, was within the Supreme Court itself: Justice Antonin Scalia.

Scalia often found himself at odds with O'Connor's approach to the law. "I don't think a judge is supposed to come up with the best result," he said in an interview. "He's supposed to come up with the result that the law demands."[4] O'Connor typically stood her ground against

Scalia, and more often than not won the votes of the majority of her fellow justices.

In a 2001 *New York Times* article, George Washington University law professor Jeffrey Rosen wrote, "By her refusal to commit herself to consistent principles, O'Connor forces the court and those who follow it to engage in a guessing game about her wishes in case after case."[5] Unlike, say, the retired Justice Brennan, whose vote and reasoning were consistently liberal, or Justice Scalia, whose vote and reasoning were consistently conservative, O'Connor inhabited a middle ground that was neither one nor the other.

It was a middle ground, as many have observed, that came from her experience as a state legislator. Having been in a position to observe how court decisions affected state and local laws, as well as individuals, she was wary of any major shift in the law. She believed in going forward no further than was necessary, and in keeping an eye out for the possibility of additional change down the road. This was a philosophy that put her at odds with those on both the right and the left who wanted to move the law more quickly.

As fellow justice Stephen Breyer said in an interview with Joan Biskupic, "[O'Connor] tries to think through the consequences of saying less or saying more. And if there are great unknowns out there, she does not believe you should go further than you have to go."[6] Ironically, in the eyes of many Americans, the Supreme Court and Justice O'Connor went much further in one of the next major court decisions than many thought they should ever go.

BUSH V. GORE

When citizens go into the voting booth to cast their votes for president of the United States, they are not actually voting for their chosen candidate. There is not one national election. There are, in effect, 50 state elections. Voters are

People jam the sidewalk in front of the U.S. Supreme Court on December 11, 2000. The high court was hearing oral arguments on an appeal by Republican presidential nominee George W. Bush to stop the hand recount of presidential ballots in Florida. The court decided in favor of Bush.

in fact technically voting for a slate of "electors" who are pledged to vote for particular candidates in the Electoral College. The candidate who then receives a majority (270) of the electoral votes wins the presidential elections.

As the votes were counted in the 2000 presidential election, viewers were mesmerized as the Florida tally went first one way, then the other. The different television news stations, in a race to be the first to declare a winner in the election, attempted to call the race in Florida early. First, Democrat Al Gore was declared the winner in Florida. Then, it became too close to call. Then, the votes counted indicated that Republican George W. Bush had won the state. Because of that, despite the fact that Bush was trailing in the popular vote count nationwide, Florida's 25 electoral votes were enough to give him a majority of the Electoral College votes—271—and therefore, the presidency.

On November 8, 2000, the day after the election, the Florida Division of Elections reported that Bush had won by just 1,784 votes. According to Florida law, since the difference in the vote count was less than 0.5 percent of the total votes cast, there would be an automatic recounting of the machine vote. This recount lowered Bush's lead to a mere 327 votes. The closeness of the vote count and the fact that whoever won the state of Florida would become the next president of the United States set the stage for a series of court challenges centering on one question: Should there be a manual recount of all the votes in the Florida counties where the vote tallies were in serious doubt?

The Bush campaign argued that the vote count had been fair and legal, and that any recounting done was unnecessary and illegal. The Gore team argued that until every vote was accurately counted, the validity of the vote count was in question. The arguments went back and forth, even as the four counties in question had in fact begun counting by hand each and every vote cast. On November 26, 2000, Florida Secretary of State Katherine Harris announced that the deadline for counting votes had passed, and she declared Bush the winner.

A heated legal battle between the Bush and Gore campaigns began in the courts. On December 8, 2000, the Florida Supreme Court ordered a statewide manual recount. The next day, the U.S. Supreme Court, by a vote of 5 to 4, stopped the recount. It now appeared the Supreme Court would help determine the next president.

It was not a case that Justice O'Connor had ever imagined she would hear. In fact, when questioned on the subject a few days after the election, she responded: "Oh no, it could never go to the Supreme Court. That's a state matter."[7] Yet, on December 11, oral arguments were heard at the U.S. Supreme Court on something that O'Connor had described as "a state matter."

The fact that the Supreme Court took up the matter struck some observers as somewhat surprising. The five justices who voted to hear the case were the ones who generally wanted the least amount of federal interference in state affairs. The four who voted against hearing the case were the ones who generally supported the right of the federal government to step in on state matters.

The legal questions facing the justices were these: Did the Florida court's ruling go against the constitution of the state of Florida, which gave the legislature the authority for the appointment of presidential electors? Did the Florida court's recount plan—which did not set a single standard for counting votes, but allowed it to vary from county to county—break due process and equal protection of the law? The nation, which had watched, mesmerized, for 37 days for the election controversy to be resolved, waited breathlessly for the court's decision.

Just one day after hearing oral arguments, the justices ruled 5 to 4 that the recounts could not continue. The five justices who voted in the majority—Rehnquist, O'Connor, Scalia, Kennedy, and Thomas—declared that the lack of a uniform standard for recounting the votes, in combination with acceptance of partial recounts in one county and not in others, violated the constitutional guarantees of equal protection (meaning that everybody's vote would count and be treated equally) and of due process. The election of 2000 was finally over. George W. Bush would be the nation's next president.

Curiously, the opinion added: "Our consideration is limited to the present circumstances, for the problem of equal protection in election processes generally presents many complexities." In other words, this decision to block Florida's recount was a one-time-only decision and, unlike any other court decision, could not be used in deciding any future cases. The opinion was unsigned, labeled instead as *per curiam*, which means "by the court." No single justice was identified as its author.

For many Americans, the Supreme Court's decision was correct because it ended a long, drawn-out voting process, blocked the Florida courts from interfering in what was largely a legislative process, and stopped the chaos that had been engulfing the Florida electoral process. To others, the decision was badly done. For those people, it was curious that the five judges who were the leaders in federalism—leaving the state's courts to interpret the state's laws—would jump in and second-guess Florida's decision.

The four justices who dissented were uniform in their dismay over the decision. Justice Ginsburg wrote: "Rarely has this Court rejected outright an interpretation of state law by a state high court." Justice Stevens, equally outraged, wrote in his opinion: "Although we may never know with complete certainty the identity of the winner of this year's presidential election, the identity of the loser is perfectly clear. It is the nation's confidence in the judge as an impartial guardian of the rule of law."

What particularly angered critics of the Supreme Court's decision was that the five judges who, in effect, named Republican George W. Bush as president all had been appointed by Republicans. Although politics have historically played a part in many Supreme Court decisions, the *appearance* that the justices' political beliefs played a part in their decision was, to some, too clear to ignore. O'Connor herself came under particular fire. Both *Newsweek* and the *Wall Street Journal* reported that when CBS news anchor Dan Rather announced that Florida had gone to Gore (this would change a few hours later), O'Connor had appeared visibly upset. She said, "This is terrible,"[8] and left the room in disgust. Her husband told the other guests that

O'Connor was upset because she wanted to retire, and she preferred that a Republican president be elected in 2000, so that he could name her successor.

O'Connor later disputed that account, claiming that she was upset because CBS News had called the state of Florida for Gore before all the voters on the state's West Coast had voted. Nevertheless, *Bush v. Gore* damaged O'Connor's reputation in the eyes of many. A year after the decision, O'Connor noted, "There was a great deal of criticism. It was a difficult case. It's too bad that it came up. . . . We don't enjoy being thrust into the middle of political controversy."[9]

CLOSER TO THE CENTER

Over the next couple of years, O'Connor, never a true member of the court's conservative block, found herself moving even closer toward the center. She was voting more and more often with the court's more liberal judges: Stevens, Ginsburg, Breyer, and Souter.

In 2001, for example, she made public her growing concerns about the death penalty in a speech to the Minnesota Women Lawyers Association. "After twenty years on the high court, I have to acknowledge that serious questions are being raised about whether the death penalty is being fairly administered in this country."[10] Newspapers had all recently run stories about prisoners being cleared through DNA testing, and stories of defendants receiving poor legal representation in court. These stories had raised questions in the public's mind about the essential fairness of the death penalty.

O'Connor soon found an opportunity in the Supreme Court to make her recent change of heart part of the nation's law. In one case, she voted in favor of a prisoner who argued that he had been weakly defended at his trial. In another case, she supported the suit of another

Supreme Court Justice Sandra Day O'Connor listens to remarks during the swearing-in ceremony of U.S. Attorney General Alberto Gonzales at the Department of Justice in Washington, D.C., on February 14, 2005.

prisoner who argued that his court-appointed lawyers had not thoroughly examined his prior record, which demonstrated that he had been abused as a child and that he suffered from mental health problems—both issues that could have persuaded a jury to sentence him to life in prison rather than death.

Her vote in the case of *Atkins v. Virginia* demonstrated how her thinking had evolved. In 1989, she had written the opinion in *Penry v. Lynaugh* that allowed the death penalty for mentally disabled criminals. Just 13 years later, she voted to ban capital punishment for such prisoners, joining Justice Stevens's opinion that such executions violated the Constitution's ban on cruel and unusual punishment.

What had changed for her? In part, she changed because the country had changed. When she wrote her original opinion in 1989, 16 states banned capital punishment for the mentally disabled. By 2002, that number had jumped to 30. Clearly, based on the actions of state legislatures, public opinion was changing. As always, O'Connor took that into account when making her decision.

Her opinion shifted in other cases as well. In 1986, she had signed the majority opinion in *Bowers v. Hardwick*, which stated that individual states had the right to outlaw consensual sexual relations between gay people. Then, in 2003, in the case of *Lawrence v. Texas*, she said that states could no longer outlaw same-sex sexual activity. Although her concurring opinion did not go as far as Justice Kennedy's majority opinion in arguing the right of privacy, her vote did ensure that states could not pass laws aimed against gay men and women.

DRAWING TO A CLOSE

In 2002, O'Connor, along with her brother Alan, wrote a memoir titled *Lazy B*, which described in loving detail their life growing up on the ranch. After the book became a nationwide best-seller, O'Connor went on to write two additional books, *The Majesty of the Law: Reflections of a Supreme Court Justice* and *Chico*, a children's book about her favorite horse on the Lazy B. She also traveled during this time, involving herself in the international legal scene and giving lectures. Yet the center of her professional life remained on the Supreme Court, and she still didn't hesitate to take the lead in a number of controversial cases.

In the cases of *Grutter v. Bollinger* and *Gratz v. Bollinger*, which involved affirmative action to encourage diversity on the campus of the University of Michigan, O'Connor again struck a middle ground for the Supreme Court. In her opinion, she upheld the school's program, which took the applicant's race into account during the admission process. At the same time, she limited her endorsement to the here and now, stating that such programs hopefully would not be necessary in 25 years.

New challenges for the Supreme Court arose in the wake of the terrorist attacks against the United States on September 11, 2001. Following those attacks and the U.S. invasion of Afghanistan that followed, the Bush administration claimed that the president had the power to imprison anyone captured in a war zone, to label them "enemy combatants," and to hold them for an open-ended amount of time.

In the case of *Hamdi v. Rumsfeld*, O'Connor took a leading role in striking down those policies. Yaser Esam Hamdi had been born in Louisiana, grew up in Saudi Arabia, and was captured with Taliban fighters in Afghanistan in late 2001. Since then he had been labeled an enemy combatant by the administration and held in an army prison center in South Carolina. Hamdi claimed through his father that he was in Afghanistan as a relief worker, not as a fighter, but without access to the court system, he was powerless to defend himself. His father, therefore, filed a habeas corpus petition on his son's behalf.

Eight members of the Supreme Court voted in favor of Hamdi, stating that the executive branch does *not* have the power to hold a U.S. citizen in prison for an unstated amount of time without the basic due process protections offered to every citizen. O'Connor, writing for the majority, noted that a U.S. citizen, regardless of being labeled an enemy combatant, had the right to due process of law, to be told of the charges against him, and to be able to argue his innocence in front of a neutral judge or military court. "History and common sense teach us that an unchecked system of detention carries the potential to become a means for oppression and abuse," she wrote.[11]

Even after more than 20 years on the court, O'Connor, with this opinion, continued to surprise her critics, standing on legal principle and her own sense of legal right and wrong. She was at the peak of her influence and power. Therefore, it came as a shock to nearly everyone when, on July 1, 2005, O'Connor announced that she would be retiring from the Supreme Court.

Life After
the Court

The news came as a surprise to the nation—and even to her fellow justices on the Supreme Court. In fact, Justice Scalia said that he had heard the news on the radio on his drive into work. Why would O'Connor decide that now was the time for retirement?

O'Connor came to her decision to retire from the bench for the most personal of reasons: to take care of John O'Connor, her husband of 53 years, who had been diagnosed with Alzheimer's disease five years earlier. Alzheimer's, the most common form of dementia, appears in its earliest stage with symptoms such as memory loss. As the disease advances, victims may display new symptoms, such as confusion, irritability, aggression, mood swings, inability to use language, long-term memory loss, and a general withdrawal from the world around them. Finally, bodily functions weaken, ultimately leading to the patient's death. As a disease with no known cure, it is a particularly difficult one for the patient's family to endure.

For O'Connor, whose husband had given up his own career in Arizona to accompany her to Washington, it was time for her to sacrifice her career for him. She would leave the Supreme Court so that she could take care of him and be with him as much as possible. It must have been particularly painful for O'Connor to watch her husband slowly exhibit signs of Alzheimer's disease, since her own mother had suffered from the same illness. But if so, she never showed it publicly. For five years, she did what she could do to help him maintain a public life for as long as possible. As always, work had been her refuge, the way that she helped manage and keep some control over her own life.

Finally, it became clear to O'Connor that she would have to leave the court to take care of her husband full-time. On July 19, President Bush nominated D.C. Circuit Judge John G. Roberts Jr., to succeed her. O'Connor heard the news on her car radio while returning from a fishing trip, and she felt that Roberts was a highly qualified choice. Still, she couldn't help but be disappointed that her replacement was not a woman. Justice Ginsburg would now be the court's only female justice.

O'Connor had planned to leave the Supreme Court before the next term started on October 3, 2005. But then, on September 3, O'Connor's longtime friend and colleague Chief Justice Rehnquist died. Two days later, President Bush withdrew Roberts as his nominee for O'Connor's seat and instead appointed him to fill the office of chief justice. O'Connor would remain on the court until her replacement could be confirmed.

On October 3, President Bush nominated White House Counsel Harriet Miers to replace O'Connor. On October

Sandra Day O'Connor gives a speech at the Kerr Cultural Center in Scottsdale, Arizona, on February 1, 2006, her first day of retirement from the Supreme Court.

27, facing a storm of opposition from critics on all sides of the political spectrum over her lack of qualifications, Miers asked Bush to withdraw her nomination. He did so the same day. On October 31, the president nominated Third Circuit Judge Samuel Alito to replace O'Connor. Alito was confirmed and sworn in on January 31, 2006. Five days earlier, O'Connor had delivered her final opinion from the bench of the Supreme Court, announcing a unanimous decision in the case of *Ayotte v. Planned Parenthood of Northern New England*. With that, her career as the nation's first female justice on the Supreme Court ended.

She would have preferred to stay. She loved the work, the challenge, being at the center of the action. She wanted, like most other justices, to work until she died or became unable to work. "Most of them get ill and are really in bad shape, which I would've done at the end of the day myself, I suppose, except my husband was ill and I needed to take action there."[1]

AFTER THE COURT

For months after leaving the Supreme Court, O'Connor did her best to take care of her husband herself, but it soon became clear that his health had worsened to the point where she could no longer do it alone. Reluctantly, she and her sons placed him in a health center in Phoenix specializing in the care of Alzheimer's patients.

As her husband's memories of her and their life together faded, O'Connor found herself facing a situation not altogether uncommon in the families of Alzheimer's patients. In November 2007, it was revealed by the couple's oldest son, Scott, that his father was no longer able to remember his life with his wife, and had fallen in love with someone else, a fellow patient at the care center.

Somewhat surprisingly, according to Scott, his mother was happy about the situation. "Mom was thrilled that

Members of the Iraq Study Group arrive on Capitol Hill for a news conference about the group's report on December 6, 2006. From left to right are Alan Simpson, William Perry, Charles Robb, Sandra Day O'Connor, James Baker, Lee Hamilton, Edwin Meese, Vernon Jordan, and Leon Panetta.

Dad was relaxed and happy and comfortable living here and wasn't complaining," Scott told KPNX–Channel 12 in Phoenix. Scott went on to compare his father to "a teenager in love," and said that, "For Mom to visit when he's happy . . . visiting with his girlfriend, sitting on the porch swing holding hands,"[2] was a relief after a painful period.

O'Connor began dividing her time between visiting her husband and family in Phoenix, and going to Washington, D.C., where, as a retired judge, she is allowed to maintain offices in the Supreme Court Building. She remains busy giving speeches and lectures, and she was part of the 10-member Baker-Hamilton Commission, appointed by

Congress on March 15, 2006, to assess the ongoing war in Iraq and to give policy recommendations.

She also has become a tireless advocate for additional research and aid to help fight Alzheimer's disease. She addressed the Senate's Special Committee on Aging on May 14, 2008: "Our nation certainly is ready to get deadly serious about this deadly disease," she said. "My beloved husband John suffers from Alzheimer's. He is not in very good shape at present."[3]

O'Connor has continued to make her opinions known on other causes as well, speaking out about the attacks on an independent judiciary by some members of Congress and state legislatures, as well as by private interest groups. In an effort to help broaden the nation's understanding of the importance of the courts, she is helping to develop a Web site and interactive civics curriculum for seventh, eighth, and ninth graders called Our Courts (http://www. ourcourts.org). "We'll have them arguing real issues, real legal issues, against the computer and against each other,"[4] she said at the Games for Change conference. As an example, she said that one of the first interactive activities would make students realize the importance of First Amendment issues by asking questions about the ability of public schools to censor student's free speech in student newspapers, for example, or on T-shirts. "Knowledge about our government is not handed down through the gene pool," she said. "Every generation has to learn it, and we have some work to do."[5]

HER LEGACY

As the first woman to sit on the U.S. Supreme Court, Sandra Day O'Connor is guaranteed a place in the nation's history books. But her legacy goes beyond just being "first." She made a mark on the court and on the nation's laws in

Sandra Day O'Connor (*left*) and former Speaker of the House Newt Gingrich testify about Alzheimer's disease before the Senate Special Committee on Aging on Capitol Hill on May 14, 2008.

ways that are still being revealed. As the *New York Times* said in an editorial upon her retirement:

> She was sometimes called the most powerful person in America. That seems like a huge overbilling for a woman who toiled at legal writing in a modest office with a small staff, and whose vote was only one of nine. But on issue after crucial issue, it was her swing vote that decided what kind of nation America would be. Justice O'Connor's America is one that hews to conservative principles, but it is tempered by a compassion for individuals and an unwillingness to follow ideology blindly to unreasonable places.[6]

The editorial went on to discuss the kind of judge that the president should select to replace O'Connor, saying that if the nation is lucky, "the president will understand how much he owes this quiet jurist who consistently looked for common ground."[7] By constantly looking for common ground, Sandra Day O'Connor became the most influential Supreme Court justice of modern times. The young, ambitious cowgirl from the Lazy B had done herself, her parents, and her nation proud.

CHRONOLOGY

1930   Born Sandra Day in El Paso, Texas, on March 26. Spends her early years at her family's ranch on the Arizona–New Mexico border.

1946   After attending Radford School for Girls, graduates from El Paso's Austin High School.

1950   Graduates magna cum laude from Stanford University.

1952   Graduates third in class from Stanford Law School. Marries John Jay O'Connor III. Becomes deputy county attorney in San Mateo, California.

1954   Begins two years as civilian lawyer for U.S. Army in Frankfurt, West Germany.

1957   Gives birth to her first of three sons, Scott Hampton O'Connor. Opens own law practice with Tom Tobin in a strip shopping mall.

1960   Gives birth to her second son, Jay O'Connor. Spends next five years as a stay-at-home mother and working for the Republican Party and other civic groups.

1962   Gives birth to her youngest son, Brian O'Connor.

1965   Appointed Arizona assistant attorney general.

1969   Appointed to Arizona State Senate.

1970   Elected to first of two full terms in state senate.

1973   Becomes senate majority leader.

1975   Elected judge of Arizona Superior Court.

1979   Appointed by Democrat Governor Bruce Babbitt to Arizona Court of Appeals.

1981   Nominated by President Ronald Reagan to U.S. Supreme Court. Confirmed by U.S. Senate in September, and sworn in as country's first female associate justice on September 25.

1982   Hears cases of *Enmund v. Florida* and *Mississippi University for Women v. Hogan*.

1985   Hears case of *Garcia v. San Antonio Metropolitan Transit Authority*.

1988   Learns that she has breast cancer; given a clean bill of health after surgery and treatment.

1989   Hears cases of *Teague v. Lane, Penry v. Lynaugh*, and *Webster v. Reproductive Health Services*.

1991   Hears case of *Coleman v. Thompson*.

1992   Hears case of *Planned Parenthood of Southeastern Pennsylvania v. Casey*.

2000   Hears case of *Bush v. Gore*.

2002   Hears case of *Atkins v. Virginia*. Writes memoir of her childhood in the Southwest, titled *Lazy B*.

2005   Retires from the U.S. Supreme Court to take care of her husband, who is suffering from Alzheimer's disease.

NOTES

CHAPTER 1: BECOMING THE FIRST

1. Stanton Abramson, "The Supreme Court in the Balance," *The Emory Wheel*, September 25, 2008. Available online at http://emorywheel.com/detail-pf.php?n=25869.
2. Joan Biskupic, *Sandra Day O'Connor: How the First Woman on the Supreme Court Became Its Most Influential Justice*. New York: HarperCollins, 2005, p. 71.
3. Ibid., p. 3.
4. Ibid., p. 2.
5. Ibid., p. 4.
6. Ibid., p. 77.
7. Ronald Reagan, "Remarks Announcing the Intention to Nominate Sandra Day O'Connor to Be an Associate Justice of the United States," July 7, 1981. Available online at http://www.presidency.ucsb.edu/ws/index.php?pid=44042.
8. Charles Lane, "In the Center, Hers was the Vote that Counted," *Washington Post*, July 2, 2005. Available online at http://www.washingtonpost.com/wp-dyn/content/article/2005/07/01/AR2005070101087.html.

CHAPTER 2: LIFE ON THE RANCH

1. Sandra Day O'Connor and H. Alan Day, *Lazy B: Growing Up On a Cattle Ranch in the American Southwest*. New York: Random House, 2002, p. 5.
2. Ibid., p. 25.
3. Biskupic, *Sandra Day O'Connor*, p. 13.
4. O'Connor and Day, *Lazy B*, p. 34.
5. Biskupic, *Sandra Day O'Connor*, p. 8.
6. Ibid., p. 17.
7. Ibid., p. 18.
8. O'Connor and Day, *Lazy B*, p. 243.

9. Scott Bales, "In Honor of Sandra Day O'Connor: Justice Sandra Day O'Connor: No Insurmountable Hurdles," *Stanford Law Review*, May 12, 2006. Available online at http://lawreview.stanford.edu/content/vol58/issue6/bales.pdf.

CHAPTER 3: TRYING TO GET THROUGH THE DOOR

1. Charles Lane, "The Professor Who Lit the Spark," *Stanford Magazine*, January/February 2006. Available online at http://www.stanfordalumni.org/news/magazine/2006/janfeb/features/spark.html.
2. Biskupic, *Sandra Day O'Connor*, p. 24.
3. Erin Wiley, "An Interview with Justice O'Connor," November 18, 2007. Available online at http://ms-jd.org/interview-justice-o039connor.
4. Biskupic, *Sandra Day O'Connor*, p. 26.
5. Ibid., pp. 6–27.
6. O'Connor and Day, *Lazy B*, p. 285.
7. Richard Sisson, Christian Zacher, and Andrew Cayton, eds., *The American Midwest: An Interpretive Encyclopedia*. Bloomington: Indiana University Press, 2007, p. 1588.
8. Pat Smith, "Magazine Cupid for Lawyer Couple," *Arizona Republic*, September 27, 1957.

CHAPTER 4: MAKING HER NAME

1. Wiley, "An Interview with Justice O'Connor."
2. Biskupic, *Sandra Day O'Connor*, p. 34.
3. Ibid., p. 35.
4. Sandra Day O'Connor, *The Majesty of the Law: Reflections of a Supreme Court Justice*. New York: Random House, 2003, pp. 200–201.
5. Biskupic, *Sandra Day O'Connor*, p. 39.

6. Ibid., p. 55.
7. Ibid., p. 56.
8. Bales, "In Honor of Sandra Day O'Connor."
9. Bernie Wynn, "A Woman May Lead Arizona Senate GOP," *Arizona Republic*, November 12, 1972.
10. Bill Mears, "35 years after Roe: A legacy of law and morality," CNN, January 21, 2008. Available online at http://www.cnn.com/2008/US/01/21/scotus.roevwade/index.html.
11. Ibid.
12. Peter Huber, *Sandra Day O'Connor: Supreme Court Justice*. New York: Chelsea House, 1990, p. 40.
13. Biskupic, *Sandra Day O'Connor*, p. 62.

CHAPTER 5: MOVING UP
1. Biskupic, *Sandra Day O'Connor*, p. 65.
2. Linda Kauss, "A Day in Court with Judge Sandra O'Connor," *Phoenix Gazette*, September 18, 1975.
3. Edythe Jensen, "Tearful Scene in Courtroom: Realtor, Mother of Two Given Prison Term on Check Forgeries," *Phoenix Gazette*, August 2, 1978.
4. Huber, *Sandra Day O'Connor*, p. 46.
5. Biskupic, *Sandra Day O'Connor*, p. 80.
6. B. Drummond Ayres Jr., "'A Reputation for Excelling': Sandra Day O'Connor," *New York Times*, July 8, 1981. Available online at http://www.nytimes.com/1981/07/08/national/08OCON.html.
7. Biskupic, *Sandra Day O'Connor*, pp. 1–82.
8. *The Nation*, editorial reprinted in "For the Record," *Washington Post*, September 18, 1981.
9. O'Connor, *The Majesty of the Law*, pp. xiii–xiv.
10. Ibid., p. xii.
11. Biskupic, *Sandra Day O'Connor*, p. 92.
12. Ibid., p. 93.

13. Ibid., p. 95.
14. Richard Stengel, with Evan Thomas, "A New Order in the Court," *Time*, October 5, 1981. Available online at http://www.time.com/time/magazine/article/0,9171,921049,00.html.

CHAPTER 6: NEW WOMAN ON THE COURT
1. O'Connor, *The Majesty of the Law*, p. 3.
2. Biskupic, *Sandra Day O'Connor*, pp. 106–107.
3. Pam Hait, "Sandra Day O'Connor: Warm, Witty and Wise," *Ladies' Home Journal*, April 1982, p. 40.
4. Biskupic, *Sandra Day O'Connor*, p. 112.
5. Ibid., p. 127.
6. Ibid., p. 128.

CHAPTER 7: MAKING HER MARK
1. Biskupic, *Sandra Day O'Connor*, p. 144.
2. Ibid., pp. 145–146.
3. "And Now, the Arizona Twins," *Time*, April 19, 1982. Available online at http://www.time.com/time/magazine/article/0,9171,950648,00.html.
4. Biskupic, *Sandra Day O'Connor*, pp. 160–161.
5. *Garcia v. San Antonio Metropolitan Transit Authority*, 469 U.S. 528 (1985).

CHAPTER 8: FINDING A MIDDLE GROUND
1. Biskupic, *Sandra Day O'Connor*, p. 187.
2. Huber, *Sandra Day O'Connor*, p. 99.
3. Biskupic, *Sandra Day O'Connor*, p. 190.
4. Ibid., p. 191.
5. Ibid., p. 209.
6. "The 'Christian Nation' Controversy," *American Lawyer*, June 1989, p. 70.
7. Biskupic, *Sandra Day O'Connor*, p. 211.

8.   Ibid., p. 230.
9.   Ibid.
10.   Ibid., p. 231.
11.   *Hodgson v. Minnesota*, 497 U.S. 417 (1990).
12.   *Coleman v. Thompson*, 501 U.S. 722 (1991).
13.   "Federalism, Despoiled," *New York Times*, June 27, 1991.
14.   Biskupic, *Sandra Day O'Connor*, p. 246.

CHAPTER 9: THE MOST POWERFUL WOMAN IN THE NATION

1.   Biskupic, *Sandra Day O'Connor*, p. 257.
2.   Joan Biskupic, "High Court's Justice With a Cause: Bench Position Amplifies Ginsburg's Lifelong Feminist Message," *Washington Post*, April 17, 1995.
3.   Howard Kohn, "Front and Center: On a Changing Supreme Court, Sandra Day O'Connor Has Emerged as a New Power, Especially on the Issue that Will Not Go Away: Abortion," *Los Angeles Times Magazine*, April 18, 1993.
4.   Biskupic, *Sandra Day O'Connor*, p. 278.
5.   Jeffrey Rosen, "A Majority of One," *New York Times Magazine*, June 3, 2001.
6.   Biskupic, *Sandra Day O'Connor*, p. 288.
7.   Ibid., p. 303.
8.   Ibid., p. 308.
9.   NBC News, Dateline transcript, January 25, 2002.
10.   Biskupic, *Sandra Day O'Connor*, p. 319.
11.   *Hamdi v. Rumsfeld*, 542 U.S. 507 (2004).

CHAPTER 10: LIFE AFTER THE COURT

1.   "Former Justice O'Connor: 'I Would Have Stayed Longer,'" NewsMax.com Wires, February 5, 2007.

Available online at http://archive.newsmax.com/archives/articles/2007/2/5/92619.shtml.

2. Joan Biskupic, "A new page in O'Connors' love story," *USA Today*, November 13, 2007. Available online at http://www.usatoday.com/news/nation/2007-11-12-court_N.htm.

3. "O'Connor Makes Personal Plea for Alzheimer's Aid," ABC News, May 14, 2008. Available online at http://abcnews.go.com/Politics/wireStory?id=4851252.

4. Seth Schiesel, "Former Justice Promotes Web-Based Civics Lessons," *New York Times*, June 9, 2008. Available online at http://www.nytimes.com/2008/06/09/arts/09sand.html.

5. Ibid.

6. "Justice O'Connor," *New York Times*, July 2, 2005. Available online at http://www.nytimes.com/2005/07/02/opinion/02sat1.html?_r=1&oref=slogin.

7. Ibid.

BIBLIOGRAPHY

ABC News. "O'Connor Makes Personal Plea for Alzheimer's Aid." May 14, 2008. Available online at http://abcnews.go.com/Politics/wireStory?id=4851252.

Abramson, Stanton. "The Supreme Court in the Balance." *Emory Wheel*, September 25, 2008. Available online at http://emorywheel.com/detail-pf.php?n=25869.

American Lawyer. "The 'Christian Nation' Controversy." June 1989, p. 70.

Ayres, B. Drummond, Jr. "'A Reputation for Excelling': Sandra Day O'Connor." *New York Times*, July 8, 1981. Available online at http://www.nytimes.com/1981/07/08/national/08OCON.html.

Bales, Scott. "In Honor of Sandra Day O'Connor: Justice Sandra Day O'Connor: No Insurmountable Hurdles." *Stanford Law Review*, May 12, 2007. Available online at http://lawreview.stanford.edu/content/vol58/issue6/bales.pdf.

Biskupic, Joan. "A new page in O'Connors' love story." *USA Today*, November 13, 2007. Available online at http://www.usatoday.com/news/nation/2007-11-12-court_N.htm.

Biskupic, Joan. *Sandra Day O'Connor: How the First Woman on the Supreme Court Became Its Most Influential Justice.* New York: HarperCollins, 2005.

Coleman v. Thompson, 501 U.S. 722 (1991).

Garcia v. San Antonio Metropolitan Transit Authority, 469 U.S. 528 (1985).

Greenhouse, Linda. "O'Connor Held Balance of Power." *New York Times*, July 2, 2005. Available online at http://www.nytimes.com/2005/07/02/politics/politicsspecial1/02oconnor.html.

Hait, Pam. "Sandra Day O'Connor: Warm, Witty and Wise." *Ladies' Home Journal*, April 1982, p. 40.

Hamdi v. Rumsfeld, 548 U.S. 507 (2004).

Hodgson v. Minnesota, 497 U.S. 417 (1990).

Huber, Peter. *Sandra Day O'Connor: Supreme Court Justice*. New York: Chelsea House, 1990.

Jensen, Edythe. "Tearful Scene in Courtroom: Realtor, Mother of Two Given Prison Term on Check Forgeries." *Phoenix Gazette*, August 2, 1978.

Kauss, Linda. "A Day in Court with Judge Sandra O'Connor." *Phoenix Gazette*, September 18, 1975.

Kohn, Howard. "Front and Center: On a Changing Supreme Court, Sandra Day O'Connor Has Emerged as a New Power, Especially on the Issue that Will Not Go Away: Abortion." *Los Angeles Times Magazine*, April 18, 1993.

Lane, Charles. "The Professor Who Lit the Spark." *Stanford Magazine*, January/February 2006. Available online at http://www.stanfordalumni.org/news/magazine/2006/janfeb/features/spark.html.

Malatin, Jeff. "Women in Arizona Politics: From Suffrage to Governing." Available online at http://www.ic.arizona.edu/ic/mcbride/ws200/jeff.html.

Mears, Bill. "35 years after Roe: A legacy of law and morality." CNN, January 21, 2008. Available online at http://www.cnn.com/2008/US/01/21/scotus.roevwade/index.html.

New York Times. "Federalism, Despoiled." June 27, 1991. Available online at http://query.nytimes.com/gst/fullpage.html?res=9D0CE7DD1730F934A15755C0A967958260.

New York Times. "Justice O'Connor." July 2, 2005. Available online at http://www.nytimes.com/2005/07/02/opinion/02sat1.html?_r=1&oref=slogin.

NewsMax.com Wires. "Former Justice O'Connor: 'I Would Have Stayed Longer.'" February 5, 2007. Available online at http://archive.newsmax.com/archives/articles/2007/2/5/92619.shtml.

O'Connor, Sandra Day, and H. Alan Day. *Lazy B: Growing Up On a Cattle Ranch in the American Southwest*. New York: Random House, 2002.

O'Connor, Sandra Day. *The Majesty of the Law: Reflections of a Supreme Court Justice*. New York: Random House, 2003.

Oyez: U.S. Supreme Court Media. "Biography: Sandra Day O'Connor." Available online at http://www.oyez.org/justices/sandra_day_oconnor.

Reagan, Ronald. "Remarks Announcing the Intention to Nominate Sandra Day O'Connor To Be an Associate Justice of the United States." July 7, 1981. Available online at http://www.presidency.ucsb.edu/ws/index.php?pid=44042.

Rosen, James. "Transcript: O'Connor on FOX." FOXNews.com, July 1, 2005. Available online at http://www.foxnews.com/story/0,2933,161325,00.html.

Rosen, Jeffrey. "A Majority of One." *New York Times Magazine*, June 3, 2001.

Schiesel, Seth. "Former Justice Promotes Web-Based Civics Lessons." *New York Times*, June 9, 2008. Available online at http://www.nytimes.com/2008/06/09/arts/09sand.html.

Sisson, Richard, Christian Zacher, and Andrew Cayton, eds. *The American Midwest: An Interpretive Encyclopedia*. Bloomington: Indiana University Press, 2007.

Smith, Pat. "Magazine Cupid for Lawyer Couple." *Arizona Republic*, September 27, 1957.

Stengel, Richard, with Evan Thomas. "A New Order in the Court." *Time*, October 5, 1981. Available online at http://www.time.com/time/magazine/article/0,9171,921049,00.html.

Stritof, Sheri, and Bob Stritof. "John and Sandra Day O'Connor Marriage Profile." About.com. Available online at http://marriage.about.com/od/politics/p/sandraoconnor.htm.

Time. "And Now, the Arizona Twins." Available online at http://www.time.com/time/magazine/article/0,9171,950648,00.html.

Washington Post. "*The Nation* editorial, reprinted in 'For the Record.'" September 18, 1981.

Wiley, Erin. "An Interview with Justice O'Connor." November 18, 2007. Available online at http://ms-jd.org/interview-justice-o039connor.

Wynn, Bernie. "A Woman May Lead Arizona Senate GOP." *Arizona Republic*, November 12, 1972.

FURTHER RESOURCES

BOOKS

Amar, Akhil Reed. *America's Constitution: A Biography*. New York: Random House, 2005.

Greenburg, Jan Crawford. *Supreme Conflict: The Inside Story of the Struggle for Control of the United States Supreme Court*. New York: Penguin, 2008.

Sergis, Diana K. *Bush v. Gore: Controversial Presidential Election Case*. Berkeley Heights, N.J.: Enslow Publishers, 2003.

Toobin, Jeffrey. *The Nine: Inside the Secret World of the Supreme Court*. New York: Anchor, 2008.

INDEX

A

abortion
  legal cases, 47–49, 56, 82,
    88–93, 98–99
  Minnesota law, 91–93
  Missouri law, 88–91
  Pennsylvania law, 98–99
  record on, 56, 58–59
Alito, Samuel, 114
Arizona Appeals Court, 11
  appointment to, 53
Arizona Republic, 38, 46
Arizona State Senate, 44–46, 49,
  70
Armstrong, Anne, 46
Armstrong, Jeanette, 72
Armstrong, Sampson, 72
Atkins v. Virginia, 108
Austin High School, 23
*Ayotte v. Planned Parenthood of
  Northern New England*, 114
Ayres, B. Drummond, Jr., 55

B

Babbitt, Bruce, 53
Baker-Hamilton Commission,
  115–116
Bales, Scott, 26
Bendheim, Alice, 52
Biskupic, Joan
  interviews, 54, 67, 70, 88,
    93–94, 97, 101
  *Sandra Day O'Connor: How the
    First Woman on the Supreme
    Court Became Its Most Influ-
    ential
  Justice*, 12, 21–22, 33, 45,
    77–78, 80
Blackmun, Harold
  and the Supreme Court,
    47–48, 67, 72–73, 76, 78–80,
    88–89, 91, 99
Bork, Robert, 82
Bowers v. Hardwick, 108
Bradley, Joseph P., 36
Bradwell, Myra, 36
Brennan, William
  and the Supreme Court, 67, 72,
    75–76, 78, 89, 91, 93–95, 101
Breyer, Stephen
  and the Supreme Court, 101,
    106

Brown v. Board of Education, 7–8,
  69
Burger, Warren
  and the Supreme Court, 11,
    54, 61, 66, 71, 73, 75, 79,
    81
Burgess, Isabel, 44
Bush, George H.W.
  administration, 84, 97
Bush, George W., 8
  2000 election, 101–106
  administration, 109, 112, 114
Bush v. Gore, 8, 101–106

C

Civil Rights Movement, 8
  leaders, 68–69, 95
Clinton, Bill, 12, 100
Coleman, Roger Keith, 94–95
Coleman v. Thompson, 94–95
Colter, Jim, 52–53
Congress, 8, 14, 65, 116
  hearings, 9
  resolutions, 49
Constitution, United States, 8,
  116
  requirements of, 54
  rights, 47–49, 54–55, 65–67,
    69, 71, 73, 76, 87, 91, 99,
    108
Court of Appeals, United States
  judges, 69, 71, 82, 96–98, 100

D

Day, Ada Mae Wilkey (mother),
  18–19, 25
  Alzheimer's disease, 77, 112
  death, 86, 96
  influence of, 20–21, 23, 29
Day, Alan (brother), 23, 50, 78,
  96, 108
Day, Alice, 17
Day, Ann (sister), 23, 78
Day, Harry (father), 17–18, 28,
  50, 77
  approval, 20–21, 23, 25–26,
    29, 34–35, 95
  death, 19, 78, 96
  politics, 27
Day, Henry Clay, 17–18
Democrat Party
  leaders, 43, 53, 56, 58, 101
Denton, Jeremiah, 59

E

Electoral College, 102–104
Enmund, Earl, 72–73
Endmund v. Florida, 72–73
Engel v. Vitale, 8
Equal Rights Amendment, 10

F

Falwell, Jerry, 56
Federal Bankruptcy Court,
    42
Fennemore Craig law firm,
    38, 40, 42

G

Games for Change conference,
    116
Gideon v. Wainwright, 8
Ginsburg, Douglas, 82
Ginsburg, Ruth Bader, 36
    and the Supreme Court, 100,
        105–106, 112
Goldwater, Barry, 11, 43, 56
Gore, Al
    2000 election, 102–103,
        105–106
government, United States
    branches of, 7, 65, 70, 110
    power of, 95, 104
    wage standards, 79–80
Gratz v. Bollinger, 109
Great Depression, 20, 27, 33
Greenburg, Jan Crawford, 31
Grutter v. Bollinger, 109

H

Haig, Alexander, 77
Hamdi v. Rumsfeld, 109–110
Hamdi, Yaser Esam, 109
Harlan, John Marshall II, 45
Harris, Katherine, 103
Heard Museum of Native
    American Art, 45
Hodgson, Jane, 92
Hodgson v. Minnesota, 91
Hogan, Joe, 74–76
House of Representatives,
    56

J

Johnson, Lyndon B., 43, 69
Jordan, Barbara, 55
Judiciary Act, 65

K

Kennedy, Anthony
    and the Supreme Court, 82,
        89–90, 93, 98–99, 108
Kennedy, Cornelia, 11
Kennedy, John F., 69
Kersey, Eunice, 72–73
Kersey, Thomas, 72–73
Klein, Dempsey, 11
Kohn, Howard, 100

L

Lane, Charles, 29
Lawrence v. Texas, 108
*Lazy B: Growing Up On a Cattle
    Ranch in the American Southwest*,
    20, 26, 34–35, 108
Lazy B ranch, 18, 32, 34–35,
    37–38, 77
    childhood at, 12, 15, 17, 20,
        22, 26–28, 108, 118
    sale of, 96
Lundy, Noah, 71

M

*Majesty of the Law: Reflections of a
    Supreme Court Justice, The*, 44,
    109
Marbury v. Madison, 65
Maricopa County
    superior judgeship, 51–53
Marshall, John, 60, 65
Marshall, Thurgood
    death, 69
    and the Supreme Court, 67–
        69, 76, 89, 91, 97
Meacham, Evan, 53
Miers, Harriet, 112, 114
Miller and Chevalier law firm,
    77
*Mississippi University for Women v.
    Hogan*, 74–77
Moral Majority, 56
Murray v. Pearson, 68

N

National Association for the
    Advancement of Colored Peo-
    ple (NAACP), 68
National Coalition for Cancer
    Survivorship, 83
National Transportation Safety
    Board, 44

Nixon, Richard M.
administration, 44–46
Nofziger, Lyn, 10

O

O'Connor, Brian (son), 41
O'Connor, Jay (son), 44
O'Connor, John Jay, III (husband)
Alzheimer's disease, 111–112,
114–116
marriage, 35
meeting, 32–34
military service, 37
work of, 38, 40–42, 77, 112
O'Connor, Sandra Day
childhood, 12, 15–17, 20–23,
25–27
early work of, 36–38
education, 22–23, 27–35, 70
illness, 83–84
marriage, 35
political power of, 38, 40,
42–43, 46, 49, 86
O'Connor, Scott (son), 38, 40, 90,
114–115

P

Penry v. Lynaugh, 87, 108
Perry, David, 51
Phoenix, Arizona
History Project, 40, 43
Junior League, 42
living in, 37–38, 40, 51–52, 77
Rotary Club, 42
Pickrell, Bob, 43
*Planned Parenthood of Southeastern
Pennsylvania v. Casey*, 98
Plessy v. Ferguson, 69
Powell, Lewis
and the Supreme Court, 68,
70, 73, 76, 82
President, United States
2000 election, 101–106
appointments of justices, 9–15
Prisoner rights, 85–86
advocates, 71–72, 106
and the death penalty, 87,
94–95, 108

R

Radford School for Girls, 22–23,
28
Rathbun, Harry, 29
Rather, Dan, 105

Reagan, Nancy, 61
Reagan, Ronald, 77
administration, 9–15, 54–56,
61–62, 81–82
Reed v. Reed, 36
Reed, Thomas C., 46
Rehnquist, Nan, 38
Rehnquist, William, 38, 43
classmate, 30–32
death, 112
and the Supreme Court, 11,
31–32, 45, 61, 68, 72–73,
76, 78–79, 81–82, 89–91, 93,
98–99, 104
Republican party (GOP), 86
leaders, 10–11, 49, 51–53, 56,
82, 97, 102, 105–106
National Committee, 46
working for, 40, 42–43, 46
Riggins, John, 81
Roberts, John G., Jr., 112
Roe v. Wade
attempts to overturn, 88–91,
98–99
details of, 8, 46–49, 56, 58, 68
Roosevelt, Franklin D., 27
Rosen, Jeffrey, 101
Rose v. Lundy, 70–71

S

*Sandra Day O'Connor: How the
First Woman on the Supreme
Court Became Its Most Influential
Justice*,
(Biskupic), 12, 21–22, 33, 45,
77–78, 80
Scalia, Antonin
and the Supreme Court, 82,
90–91, 93, 100–101, 111
Senate, 8, 14
Judiciary Committee, 56–59,
82, 97, 100, 114
Special Committee on Aging,
116
September 11, 2001 terrorist
attacks, 109
Smith, William French, 9, 12, 77
Souter, David
and the Supreme Court,
96–99, 106
Stanford Law Review, 26, 32–33,
37
Stanford Law School, 29–36

Stanford University, 28, 45
Stanford v. Kentucky, 87
Starr, Kenneth, 12
Stengel, Richard, 60
Stevens, John Paul
  and the Supreme Court, 11,
    68, 76, 89, 91, 93, 99, 105–
    106, 108
Stewart, Potter, 9–10, 61
Supreme Court, United States,
  50, 53
  cases, 7–9, 36, 46–49, 56, 62–
    64, 66, 68–77, 79, 82, 84–95,
    98–99, 101–106, 108–110
  dissenting opinions, 64, 72, 80
  first female justice, 15, 54–56,
    61, 116
  judicial reviews, 65
  justices, 8–15, 31–32, 36, 45,
    47, 49, 54, 56, 58, 60–73,
    75–76, 78–82, 88–91, 93,
    96–101, 104–106,
    108, 110–112, 114
  power of, 7
  retirement from, 110–111
  workings of, 62–66, 69–70

T
Taft, William Howard, 9
Teague, Frank, 84–85

Teague v. Lane, 84–85
Thomas, Clarence, 69
  and the Supreme Court, 97,
    104
Thurmond, Strom, 59
Tobin, Tom, 40, 42

U
United Way, 42

W
Warner, Mark, 95
Webster v. Reproductive Health Ser-
  vices, 88–91, 98–99
White, Byron
  and the Supreme Court, 67,
    73, 75, 89, 93, 100
Wiley, Erin, 31
Wilkey, Mamie Scott (grand-
  mother), 18, 22–23
Wilkey, W.W., 18
Women
  discrimination against, 36,
    40–41, 46, 74–77
  rights movement, 10, 39, 56,
    75
  role in society, 31, 39, 77
World War I, 17
World War II, 30–31, 39
Wynn, Bernie, 46

ABOUT THE AUTHOR

DENNIS ABRAMS is the author of numerous books for Chelsea House, including biographies of Barbara Park, Albert Pujols, Eminem, Xerxes, Ehud Olmert, Rachael Ray, and Hillary Rodham Clinton. He attended Antioch College, where he majored in English and communications. He currently lives in Houston, Texas, with his partner of 20 years, two cats, and a dog named Junie B.

PICTURE CREDITS

Page